HO FOR CALIFORNIA!

FOR CALIFORNIA!

The Good Schooner

CIVILIAN,

170 tons, newly coppered, and four years old, Commanded by

Capt. Thomas Dodge,

of Chatham, will sail for California Oct. 20th. She is owned by the "COCHITUATE COMPANY for California," now nearly full. She is fitted up with Superior Accommodations, is a fast sailing vessel, and offers advantages equal to if not superior to any vessel that has yet been put up.

Please call for information at No. 69 Commercial Street.

Boston, Sept. 27th. 1849. **E. W. JACKSON, Agent.**

Rand & Co's Job Press, 3 Cornhill.

HO FOR CALIFORNIA!

Pioneer Women and Their Quilts

Jean Ray Laury
and
California Heritage Quilt Project

E. P. DUTTON
New York

Acknowledgments

Color photographs were taken by Sharon Risedorph and Lynn Kellner, San Francisco.

Black-and-white photographs are by courtesy of each quiltmaker's family or friends, except where noted.

CALIFORNIA HERITAGE QUILT PROJECT BOARD OF DIRECTORS:
President: Helen Gould, San Bruno; Vice President: Mary Hjalmarson, Cardiff; Recording Secretary: Jeanette Hensley, Santa Rosa; Corresponding Secretary: Virginia McElroy, Greenbrae; Treasurer, Claire Kropschot: Oakland.

Margaret Geiss-Mooney, Petaluma; Pat James, Acton; Caroline Lieberman, San Francisco; Celia LoPinto, San Francisco; Diana McClun, Walnut Creek; Kaye Rheingans, Orange; Janet Shore, El Cerrito; Mary Ann Spencer, Eureka; Sandra Walsh, Eureka; Anne Wormood, San Rafael.

ADVISORY BOARD: Sally Arnot, Eureka; Louise Bloom, Sherman Oaks; Carol Bruch, Davis; Sandi Fox, Los Angeles; Lucy Hilty, Berkeley; Roderick Kiracofe, San Francisco; Jean Ray Laury, Fresno; Judy Mathieson, Woodland Hills; Gabrielle Morris, Berkeley; Blanche Young, Middletown.

FEASIBILITY COMMITTEE 1983: Chairperson; Joyce Gross; Sue Broenkow, Cindy Dowling, Millie Faubion, Jeanette Hensley, Diane Hersh, Caroline Lieberman, Diana McClun, Patti Mills, Lyn Piercy, Janet Shore, Mary Ann Spencer, Lyn Strauch, Sandra Walsh; and special guests Katy Christopherson, Consultant, Kentucky Quilt Project, and Bettina Havig, Director, Missouri Quilt Project.

During 1985 and 1986 Quilt Search Days were held throughout the state of California. Mary Ann Spencer and Jeanette Hensley were the coordinators representing the Board. The location of each Quilt Day and the on-site coordinators are listed below. The Quilt Search Days owe their success to the help of each individual that helped at the Quilt Search Day sites. We express our gratitude and thanks for the many hours of volunteer help by hundreds of quilters and quilt lovers. The listing is in chronological order.
SACRAMENTO (#1), Lyn Strauch; SAN MATEO, Anna Brown; PACIFIC GROVE (2 days), Sue Broenkow; CHICO, Marian Graham and Pam Herman; GLENDALE, Lana Marie Wittman; SANTA ROSA, Dotty Zagar; SAN FRANCISCO (#1), Phyllis Schaefer and M.H. deYoung Museum; GARDEN GROVE and IRVINE, Blanche Young and Beverly Packard; SAN DIEGO and ESCONDIDO, Mary Hjalmarson; FRESNO, Bette Chase—Fresno Art Museum; EUREKA, Dixie McBride and Edith Goggin; REDDING, Edy Goldsworthy and John Harper—Redding Museum and Art Center; EL CERRITO and HAYWARD, Bernice Stone and Kathleen Rupley—Richmond Museum; SANTA CRUZ, Janice Brown; SAN JOSE and SANTA CLARA, Phyllis Dale; GRASS VALLEY and NEVADA CITY, Myrna Raglin; SACRAMENTO (#2), Lindy Mundy; SAN FERNANDO and SIMI VALLEY, Hannah Meottel, Sally Ann Collins, Jan Allen, Barbara Sheehan; WILLIAMS, Marilyn Ornbaun and Sacramento Valley Museum; YUBA CITY and MARYSVILLE, Cindy Brown; BAKERSFIELD, Juanita Hamilton; SAN FRANCISCO (#2), Joan Dickson and M.H. deYoung Museum; RIVERSIDE, Joan Davidson and Diana Hedrick; LOS ANGELES, Nancy McKinney—Afro-American Museum; SAN LUIS OBISPO, Marty Nelson; CAMARILLO, Sarah Beth Tennison and Pat Varnum; TURLOCK, Donna Endsley; OAKLAND, Inez Brooks Myers—Oakland Museum.

Our Quilt Search Day consultants worked long days, and we gratefully extend our appreciation to them: Charlotte Ekback, Sally Garoutte, Lucy Hilty, Rod Kiracofe, Judy Mathieson, Linda Reuther, and Board members Virginia McElroy and Jeanette Hensley.

After the Quilt Search Days were over, we moved to the next phase of the Project. We thank Selections Chairperson Virginia McElroy for coordinating the choosing of all the quilts for the book and museum; Museum Chairperson Celia LoPinto for working with the museums and arranging the venues; and Book Chairperson Caroline Lieberman for overseeing the selection of the author, publisher, and the publishing of the book.

Very special thanks go to the following people who served as consultants to the Selections Committee: Jean Ray Laury, Linda Otto Lipsett, Roderick Kiracofe, and Julie Silber for the three days spent choosing the quilts for the book.

We also want to thank the following people for all their help and assistance: Diane Baker, our pro bono attorney, and Zane Gresham of Morrison and Forester, our pro bono book attorney; Anita Barber, Cuesta Benberry, Pat Ferrero, Sandi Fox, Lucille Parker, and Bonnie Leman.

Funding for the Project came primarily from the quilt guilds and quilters of California. Their constant support made the Project a reality. We thank each individual for the many dollars contributed.

Major funding of over three thousand dollars was given to the Project by the following benefactors: San Francisco Quilters Guild, East Bay Heritage Quilters, Glendale Quilt Guild, and Orange County Quilters Guild.

We gratefully acknowledge the following grants received: California Arts Council, Hewlett Packard of Santa Rosa, The G.L. Brennen Foundation/Patricia M. Smith, American/International Quilt Association, and the Lloyd Foundation.

Another important source of income was our opportunity quilts. A wall hanging made by Lyn Piercy generated money to get us off to a good start. Jean Ray Laury and Judy Mathieson coordinated the humorous *Scenes of California* quilt made by many California quilt teachers. Blanche Young donated her lovely *Radiant Nine Patch* quilt. In 1987, Ann Albertson and a group of San Diego quilters produced the beautiful red and green *Lotus Flower* quilt. Jeanette Hensley and Caroline Lieberman coordinated the California guilds in reproducing their logos for a unique California quilt. Blanche Young donated another marvelous quilt of schoolhouses called *From a Quilter's House*. These wonderful quilts were displayed at quilt shows, guild meetings, Quilt Search Days, and quilting classes and generated keen interest and considerable money for our Project.

The Board of Directors gives very special thanks to all its family members for their financial, physical, and moral support.

We have listed as many supporters as possible. Our special thanks go to each and every person who supported this significant and exciting Project.

CALIFORNIA HERITAGE QUILT PROJECT
BOARD OF DIRECTORS

Front row (left to right): Anne Wormood, Helen Gould, Mary Hjalmarson, Jeanette Hensley. *Back row* (left to right): Celia LoPinto, Kaye Rheingans, Claire Kropschot, Meg Geiss-Mooney, Virginia McElroy, Caroline Lieberman, Janet Shore, Mary Ann Spencer. *Absent members:* Diana McClun, Sandra Walsh, Pat James.

6

Contents

Foreword

This book is about quilts and the women who made them. Their stories reflect the history of California in a unique portrayal of the "moving frontier."

Excitement generated by other quilt projects under way inspired a group of enthusiastic quilters to gather on a fall weekend in 1983 to explore the feasibility of a search for early California quilts. This book is a result of their dream. With support funds from a number of northern California quilt guilds these women agreed to explore, with the founders of the Kentucky and Missouri Quilt Projects in attendance, the goals, time frame, organization, and funding that had to be in place at the outset. At the end of three days the decision was made and the plans were set. A steering committee was elected from this group and a preliminary budget built. The purpose was documented as follows:

—to seek out and record the history of California quilts and quiltmakers
—to foster conservation and preservation of California's quilt heritage
—to increase public awareness and appreciation of quilts
—to encourage the art of quiltmaking

The feasibility study further concluded that the search would be limited to quilts made in or brought to California before 1945 (the end of World War II). This time frame would include the women and men who came to California in the massive migration triggered by the war industries that considerably changed the lifestyle and demographics of many.

Inasmuch as it had been agreed that the California Heritage Quilt Project should be statewide in scope, representatives from southern California were added at once. Within a few months two nonquilters whose skills and experience would enhance the development of the Project joined the steering committee. The Board of Directors for the California Heritage Quilt Project, a nonprofit organization, was formed in 1984.

The Project began without defined funding. Applications for grants brought little response as the goals and nature of the Project did not fit the criteria of potential grantors. It was the continuous generosity of many California quilt guilds and individual donors, along with fund-raising efforts by the Board of Directors, that saw the California Heritage Quilt Project through to its happy culmination. Quiltmaking is firmly recognized as a major form of American folk art, and the award of a matching grant by the California Arts Council in 1988 was indeed gratifying.

The Board of Directors appointed a Quilt Search Day Committee to conduct the search, and quilt owners were invited to bring their quilts for registration and dating. Quilt guilds, museums, historical societies, and educational institutions sponsored thirty-two Quilt Search Days. The search took two years because of the immense size of California, which is 825 miles in length and 345 miles at its maximum width. Local sponsors helped by finding locations, furnishing woman and manpower, "spreading the word," and providing hospitality for the Project team members, who many times traveled long distances to arrive at a Quilt Search Day location. A manual was designed for the on-site coordinator to aid in the development of a Quilt Search Day. The manual proved to be the perfect tool and has been made available to quilt projects in other states.

The Quilt Search Days were masterpieces of organization and efficiency tempered by generous doses of excitement and fun. Open to the public, Quilt Search Days attracted quilters as well as nonquilters, and participants were surprised to find such avid interest in their treasured possessions, family photographs, and stories. Many came early and stayed late watching the moving display as quilts went up and down on the frames. Each quilt owner was interviewed, and information about the quilt and its maker was carefully recorded. In turn, each quilt was displayed, then examined and dated by an expert, and then photographed. The owner received a copy of the completed quilt registration form, often the name of the quilt pattern, and information on the care and preservation of quilts. In every locale where a Quilt Search Day was held the local museums were invited to bring their quilt collections to be registered with the Project. Held in community halls, rural grange halls, museums, business facilities, and on college campuses, Quilt Search Days brought grass-roots support for the Project and importantly contributed to the quilt owners' sense of pride in their family heirlooms and brought a renewed appreciation for the tradition of quiltmaking.

Early on, the Project team began to realize that what was being learned in the interviews was testimony to the unique migration patterns of the West, especially California. It soon became clear that the focus of the Project would be a book and traveling exhibition that would provide an opportunity to share with the people of California these quilted treasures that were visual evidence of the westward movement.

Selection of the quilts to be included in the book presented a major task. Evaluated against criteria established by the Board of Directors, the selection committee met almost weekly during the summer of 1987 to cull from the 3,300 quilts seen during the thirty-two Quilt Search Days, 350 quilts for final consideration—not an easy task. A group of four experts gave generously of their time to make the final selection.

While the selection committee work was under way, two other Board committees were busy: one to select the author and publisher for the book; the other to develop museum venues. Commencing in late 1986, the three chairwomen worked as a team to plan the final stages of the Project.

Keenly aware that the information gathered about each quilt is of historic importance, the Board invited proposals for placing the material. The American Quilt Research Center of the Los Angeles County Museum of Art was chosen to house the archival material. This material will include all the information related to the organization and management of the Project since its inception in 1983.

The quilts featured in this book are obviously only a small percentage of the 3,300 quilts seen just as the 3,300 quilts are a minuscule portion of the quilts that are still unknown and unrecorded. A plan is already in motion to continue to register quilts by mail. The oldest quilt discovered by the Project dates from before 1800, while the oldest California-made quilt was dated 1850. Quilts recorded by the Project came from forty-six states in the union, five foreign countries, and the territories of Oklahoma, Dakota, and Hawaii. Thirty-seven percent were made in California and less than two percent were of unknown origin.

In conclusion, no report on this Project would be complete without commenting on the sustained interest, hard work, and vision of the fifteen volunteer members of the Board of Directors; the constant support and help of the Advisory Board; and the willingness to help of quilt guilds throughout the state.

The California Heritage Quilt Project is most grateful to:

—Jean Ray Laury, for undertaking the task of writing the text and for her sensitive relationship to the Board members whose passion for their findings is deep;

—Dr. Gloria Ricci Lothrop, whose rich background has given credence to the historical findings related to this book;

—E. P. Dutton and especially Cyril I. Nelson, for giving the California Heritage Quilt Project the opportunity to publish this book;

—Robert Barrett, director and chief curator, Fresno Art Museum, whose enthusiasm for the exhibit and whose professional acumen has encouraged this phase of the Project;

—and to all the wonderful women and men who brought to us their treasured quilts, their great stories, and the sweetness of their trust and support.

The California Heritage Quilt Project dedicates this book and the related exhibition to the people of California and to its quilts and quilt owners.

HELEN GOULD

Preface

It has been my privilege and treasured experience to get to know the 99 quilters who made the 101 quilts in this book. Not personally, of course, for some departed this earth one to two hundred years ago. But the acquaintanceships are real, and I feel I know them nevertheless.

Some of these quilters made the bedding carried by early settlers or prospectors to satisfy the crucial need for warmth and comfort. Quilts, however, satisfied another need as great as that of physical warmth: the need to feel connected to family and to other generations, the need for continuity. Quilts offered a way of maintaining ties at a time when photographs were uncommon (or unknown), and the arrival of letters by mail could take months. Quilts constituted contact. When running fingers over the quilted surface, one could sense the elusive but undeniable presence of a quiltmaker hundreds of miles away.

That any quilts survived the trip West is remarkable. It attests both to the durability of the quilts and to the loving tender care so crucial to that survival. Coming West in wagon trains, many families slept in the open, with bedding placed on the ground under or near the wagon for protection. Fear of the unknown, coupled with a fear of the known, was based on vulnerability to illness, injury, attack, wind, rain, cold, and fever. Rocky, dusty ground and drenching rains were devastating to fabrics. Births, illnesses, injuries, and deaths—all part of wagon-train life—involved the inevitable use of quilts.

Sailing to California sounds comparatively luxurious, but it, too, was difficult and expensive. Taking the Panama route involved a steamy trip across the isthmus by donkey. Extra baggage was cumbersome and costly to move. In the seemingly endless trip around the Horn (lasting from one to three hundred days), cargo and passenger space was limited. That sea-faring travelers folded quilts into their trunks attests to the values, both emotional and practical, they attached to these handmade artifacts.

The transcontinental railway eased the restrictions of moving household belongings, and later, the automobile made the move West more accessible to everyone. But selecting the family possessions to be left behind was still difficult, and automobiles had only limited space when an entire family was moving. The advent of the cross-country moving van offered the possible luxury of shipping everything (and sorting later!). As quilts came into California, they offered a kaleidoscopic view of quiltmaking throughout the United States.

We respond to a handmade quilt, even an anonymous one, in part because through it we learn about the quilter as a homemaker, caretaker, keeper of traditions, creator of intricate patterns and symbols, and as a master craftsperson. Quilts become archetypal symbols of the women who make them. They "stand in" for the quilter, long after she is gone, revealing to descendants, viewers, or new owners the essence of the quilter—her spirit, energy, vitality, and skill. While several of the quilters in this book are without names or dates, it is still possible for us to "know" them.

Westering pioneers were eager for change and looked for adventure. A few deliberately chose to break family ties in making a new start. Whether those ties were severed with regret or joy, the extended family, friends, and communities were left behind and women, especially those widowed on the hazardous trip from the East, were forced to become more independent and self-reliant. With greater responsibility came greater freedom. Unconventional, individual, and often untamed viewpoints influenced lifestyles and, ultimately, quilt design.

Many of the quilts in this cherished publication originated in California and did not have to survive the perils of travel. But no indigenous style typifies early California quilts. The diverse approaches and styles brought West were tumbled together in new communities. Diversity itself became a trait. Quilts were often pieced in order to maintain traditions and reestablish the values of a home life left behind. The quilting activity itself offered continuity, but the California move interrupted local influences on quilters' traditional work.

It is these quilters, both in and out of California, to whom I am indebted. They enabled their families to appreciate (and thus preserve) their quilts, a few of which they even signed and dated—and to those I am especially grateful!

Many friends and quilters assisted me in this project. I wish especially to thank Julie Silber, Linda Reuther, and Rod Kiracofe for their expertise, time, and humor; Sandi Fox for generously spending her entire Thanksgiving vacation with me reading manuscript; and Bea Slater, who volunteered endless hours of help. Lizabeth Laury worked with unflagging enthusiasm on maps and charts, while Jody House offered her New Year's weekend to work with me on the computer graphics. Frank Laury willingly added "house husband" to his own full schedule.

I thank Polly Mitchell of the Shellburne Museum, Cuesta Benberry, Bettina Havig, Mary Steinhauer, Sally Garoutte, the many California quilters, and my own local quilt guild, upon whom I called with alarming frequency. Thanks also to pilot Jim McElroy for flying quilts (and quilters) around the state.

Years of dedicated work and stacks of information were compiled by the Board members and all the volunteers of the California Heritage Quilt Project. They were immensely supportive and wonderful to work with, offering assistance, hospitality, and friendship at the drop of the dial tone.

Most of all, this work depended upon the quilters, their families, and the quilt owners who dug, then dug deeper, into family records, trudged through cemeteries, scanned old newspapers, and searched family Bibles or historical accounts. We have all participated in a remarkable experience, and it is our purpose and pleasure to offer the reader this opportunity to share, reflect, and be enlightened by our collective efforts.

JEAN RAY LAURY

Introduction

The road to California has been traversed by adventurers who dauntlessly crossed both land and sea. Some ventured along Indian trails; others came north from Mexico. A multitude of overlanders traveled the great heartland of the continent in pursuit of a fabled, often elusive, El Dorado. A contagious spell of wanderlust lured this army of adventurers to the Pacific shore in pursuit of gold, land, opportunity, and, sometimes, an impossible dream. As a result of this pioneer vanguard relentlessly pursuing the westward course of empire, the nation proclaimed its sovereignty from sea to sea before the United States had celebrated its first century.

The westering settlers included in their ranks a substantial complement of women about whom little is known and less has been written. History books pay scant heed to the women who, as wives and mothers, schoolmistresses, homesteaders, and entrepreneurs settled the frontier that stretched westward from the one hundredth meridian. By 1890, 936,534 women had settled in the trans-Mississippi West.

In the belief that "men make history; women simply are history," the contributions, in fact the very presence of women, have until recently been overlooked. Equally neglected has been the entire field of social history that could have surveyed the fragmentary evidence relating to these anonymous and unheralded trailblazers.

In part, this story has been obscured because of the difficulties such research poses for the conventional scholar. The stories of women are to be found shrouded in the social ephemera of a culture. Folk songs, recipe books, and tombstones are the common repositories of women's history. Testimonies contained in letters, diaries, and scrapbooks reveal the social realities of women's lives, while sermons, etiquette books, and popular literature, particularly the illustrations, convey the common expectations regarding proper female comportment. It is from these scattered sources that the pattern of women's lost history must be inferred.

Handcrafts represent a particularly rewarding area of investigation, for the needle became the most common means of creating the ornamentation that reconciled utility and art. No craft achieved this union more successfully than the uniquely indigenous American art form, the quilt.

It is true that precursors of the familiar quilt have been found in ancient tombs constructed by the First Dynasty in Egypt and also served as soft undergarments worn beneath heavy medieval armor. But the quilt is an American tradition. One of the earliest examples of the quiltmaker's art represented in this volume is the eighteenth-century blue-resist quilt that was brought to California in the 1880s.

Quilts spanned the range from decorative counterpanes and coverlets to the functional for family and hired hands. They were made from a variety of materials ranging from homespun fabrics or sugar and flour sacks to such sentimental remnants of family history as bridal gowns, baby clothes, and men's cravats. These sometimes appeared in Crazy quilts made up of thousands of pieces. Recycled remnants gleaned from the ever-present scrap bag made true the frontier adage that although "women die, their clothing lives after them."

These uniquely personal artistic creations sometimes marked births or anniversaries and often served as solemn recognition of betrothals. There were also Widows' quilts and Friendship quilts that, like those in this volume, often bore scriptural verses and well-wishers' greetings. Quilts were also created to commemorate significant historic events. This text includes one that celebrates Charles Lindbergh's transatlantic flight, and others mark the completion of the Mount Wilson Observatory near Pasadena, California, and the 1933 Century of Progress Exposition in Chicago.

Quilts, which were only occasionally dated or signed, are the most anonymous of women's traditional art forms. But historians are not satisfied with simply identifying the names of these domestic artists, who created optical illusions without training in geometry and who conjured exotic images having rarely ventured far from home or hearth. It is also important to understand that with their needles women were able to express the poignant memories as well as the intense aspirations they were often too shy to articulate publicly. Furthermore, the variety and the continuing evolution of their patterns testify to the creativity and originality of generations of quilting women.

Too often the naïve aspect of this familiar folk expression obscures the level of the art represented and regrettably belies the social history reflected. Quilts are, in sum, incomparable documentary artifacts that reflect the time during which they were made as well as revealing much about the makers themselves.

In keeping with the quilters' tradition, interpreters of women's lost history must construct from the remnant scraps of evidence, from the fragmentary threads of personal history, a social context in which the patterns of their lives emerge and women's values—their sense of order and aesthetic, their generosity, and their hope for the future—can be discerned. Quilts constitute an incomparable source of information. The California Heritage Quilt Project has compiled just such a documentary history of women who came to the Golden State. The result is an unprecedented record of migration to the Pacific slope by women representing various classes, ethnic groups, and time periods.

The land along the Pacific slope, first colonized by Hispanics and later by American settlers, had for many centuries been home to native Americans. Their lives were inexorably altered, however, when in 1769, nearly three hundred years after Juan Rodriguez Cabrillo first explored the California coast, Spain established a colony along the distant edge of its vast empire. Within a few decades missions, presidios, pueblos, and ranchos edged the California coast. The economy of these isolated outposts was sustained by a thriving cattle trade with New England merchants. A number of those seafaring "Boston men," as they were called, married Californianas. Among them was Thomas Wrightington, who in 1840 married Juana Machado Alipáz of San Diego. Included in this volume is her quilt with its striking red-and-white design accented by a running border, which reflects a local mastery of a traditional American art form, and thus a gradual blending of the two cultures.

By 1841, two wagon trains had penetrated the isolated Mexican province of Alta California. The Workman-Rowland party followed a southerly route to Mission San Gabriel, while the Bidwell-Bartleson wagon train crossed the Sierras at the Truckee Pass in order to reach the Sacramento–San Joaquin Valley. Both caravans had penetrated California's seemingly inaccessible perimeter of mountains and desert. The presence of these innocent migrants portended an end to California's insularity and marked the beginning of a pioneer cavalcade to California.

Both wagon trains included women and children, the pioneer vanguard of countless westering families whose numbers would multiply after American acquisition of California in 1848 and the discovery of gold by James Marshall in that same year. The response worldwide to the tantalizing promise of gold soon transformed California. While men, mostly young and inexperienced, constituted ninety percent of the population of gold-seeking argonauts, wives and mothers as well as resourceful entrepreneurs also converged on California in pursuit of the proverbial pot of gold.

Some of the women arrived by sea, having sailed around Cape Horn, or taken the isthmian route. Most, however, lurched and bumped their way West in overland wagon trains. More than two hundred thousand pioneers followed the "Great Platte River Route" just in the 1850s. Along the way they were forced to brave the "dreary succession of steep hills, flat alkali plains, poor water and clouds of dust." During the trek that averaged six months, the women learned to adapt to the lack of privacy and to the confinement of the wagons that lumbered along at a pace of ten to fifteen miles a day. They mastered the art of cooking over camp fires fueled with buffalo chips seasoned with sage, prepared jerked meat and hoe cake, and traded trinkets for fresh vegetables along the trail.

Most painful for these women were the pangs of separation from familiar faces and environments. The typical western pattern of settlement was in three stages, moving from the Atlantic seaboard to the Mississippi Valley and thence farther westward. Each removal meant the severing of warm friendships, a fact reflected in the number of Friendship quilts included in this text. In addition to capturing the poignancy of separation, the quilts themselves provide evidence of the migratory patterns. New England designs like the Nine Patch and Diamond patterns were gradually modified by new contacts. A Double Wedding Ring quilt in this book, to which cattle brands have been added, epitomizes this metamorphosis.

Unprepared for the arduousness of the journey, the inexperienced pioneers were often obliged to lighten loads on their wagons as they approached the last and most difficult segments of the overland route. As a result, the trail was littered with personal belongings cast off without regard for need or sentimental value. One doleful pioneer was forced to abandon her precious cargo of quilts, leaving them by the trail with the invitation to other overlanders to help themselves to "five good quilts."

For some women, the journey offered a release from the relentless toil of frontier life that wore away all but the basic need to survive. In contrast, the restricted responsibilities of wagon-train life permitted some women to socialize and even do handwork. An example included here was pieced in a covered wagon during a journey west in 1859.

Although the placer deposits were depleted soon after California was admitted to statehood in 1850, the seekers of El Dorado remained. Sacramento and San Francisco became cosmopolitan centers of commerce, while the rural areas prospered with the cultivation of wheat, hay, rice, and fruit. The vigor of the agricultural economy was reinforced by the arrival of the railroad. The linking of a transcontinental railroad in 1869, the same year as the completion of the Suez Canal, did not result in immediate prosperity for the West. But the construction of subsidiary railroads, including lines to southern California, gave a boost to citrus growers and brought an avalanche of health seekers, commonly referred to as "one lungers," to the spas and seaside resorts of the Pacific coast. A number of quilts in this volume were carried by such health-seeking pilgrims.

In March 1887, competition between the Southern Pacific and Santa Fe railroads briefly drove the fare from Kansas City to California down to one dollar. The resulting influx of residents in pursuit of a new Eden has been described as the great "boom of the 1880s." Instant cities emerged. Long Beach, Alhambra, Pomona, and Azusa became home to transcontinental migrants who brought with them their most prized possessions including two Album quilts illustrated here: one commemorates the Civil War; the other is a tribute to a fallen hero of the war with Mexico.

Westering women quickly assumed more active roles in the new, growing communities. Not only was their labor needed and welcomed but also societies removed from kinship networks and established traditions relied on women to maintain continuity with a way of life that had been left behind. Women accepted responsibilities as "city builders," establishing free kindergartens, temperance organizations, and philanthropic organizations. During the Civil War, the women of San Francisco staged one of the many sanitary fairs organized to raise funds for medical supplies for Union troops. Soon after, Adah McKelvey organized a quilting bee to honor the widow of abolitionist John Brown. The quilt, included in this volume, contains the signatures of the thirty women who participated.

Women's increasingly public role led them to articulate demands for social and political reform as evidenced in the political sentiments expressed in several quilts in this volume. By the turn of the century, calls for child-labor reforms, a minimum wage, and pure food and drug laws were echoed by the growing ranks of California progressives whose platform would soon sweep the nation. Strong-minded women, who had long toiled beside their menfolk and who had also been designated the moral guardians of society, soon understood that they could not discharge their sweeping social responsibilities as long as they were unenfranchised. To achieve this goal they recognized the importance of organization.

It was an approach familiar to women who had learned to draw support from one another at times of birth and death, and to lighten the burdensome toil of routine tasks. It was an essential verity underlying the quilting bee, which, in the words of Harriet Beecher Stowe, provided an opportunity to learn "how to bring up babies by hand;...how to reconcile absolute decrees with free will; how to make five yards of cloth answer the purpose of six; and how to put down the Democratic Party."

The tradition of the quilting bee was to continue into the twentieth century. The Red Cross quilt in this volume bears four hundred names, including the names of soldiers in World War I combat. Another joint effort lists the names of aircraft-warning personnel and their loved ones in military service during World War II.

Two widely divergent decades separated these two wars. The ebullient 1920s age of jazz, prohibition, and stock speculation was followed by the plummeting economy of the Great Depression that reached its nadir in California in 1932. By 1935, federal-aid programs were operational, but demands upon services were suddenly increased by the arrival of "exodusters," dirt farmers escaping the expanding dust bowl in Oklahoma, Arkansas, and the Texas panhandle. The ranks of the unemployed and needy swelled, the most vulnerable being the aged, whose numbers had increased in California by one hundred percent between 1920 and 1930. Proposals to ease their economic dilemma were advanced by Upton Sinclair in his EPIC campaign for governor which promised to "End Poverty in California." There were, as well, the persuasive appeals of the "Ham and Eggs" and Townsend programs. The latter plan is commemorated in one of the quilts shown here. Several other quilts reflect painful facets of the Depression decade. At least one is known to have been bartered for a tankful of gas. Another was made from ill-fitting relief-agency clothing. A third was the product of a precut, ready-to-make quilt kit marketed as a self-help effort by an unemployed couple.

The distress of the Depression was followed in the 1940s by the desolation caused by World War II. As able-bodied men were recruited for military service, women entered the work force as never before. In San Francisco alone the number of women workers grew from 138,000 in 1940 to 275,000 in 1945. Among the female riveters, welders, and metal platers, one woman employed in a Wilmington shipyard in 1943 used the wartime fabrics available to her to create the Fan quilt included in this volume.

Women defense workers contributed significantly to the armistice in 1945 that was followed by a decade of unparalleled expansion. Many of the three hundred thousand GI's who had trained in California returned to settle permanently with their families. As a result, by 1950 the state's population had reached 10,586,223, an increase of fifty-three percent from 1940. But new citizens need a greater range of social and educational services. They also constituted a work force that led in the production of aircraft, agricultural products, apparel, and communication and space technology, stimulating an economy that by 1980 ranked California fifth among the nations of the world and made the state a key partner in the emerging Pacific-rim economy.

This historic progress reflects the accomplishments of women as well as men—the contributions of women as helpmates, culture bearers, and city builders. Unfortunately, the labor, sacrifice, aspirations, and example of these women have been largely unreported in conventional commentaries, and remain to be captured in the most unexpected sources. Although they are still anonymous and their testimonies are elusive, women's passions and dreams lie hidden in their crafts. Particularly, the vibrant artistic achievement of quiltmaking provides a personal expression as well as an eloquent tribute to women's imagination and artistry. The quilters' patient commitment to detail in creating objects that are expected to endure and be cherished by subsequent generations reveal both their selflessness and their vision.

Through their quilts women have expressed both love and duty. Through them they have also conveyed what they understood of art and life. Through them we may now capture a portion of their forgotten history.

GLORIA RICCI LOTHROP
Pomona, California
January 1989

California Quilts Time Line

To place them in their historical context, this California time line relates these quilts to major events in the state's history. Bands of color identify each period of rule and its duration, starting with the year 1500. Significant political and social events appear above this band.

How quilts came to California is indicated with symbols showing the means of migration or transportation and the period of time during which each travel form was used. Covered wagons, for example, arrived from 1841 to about 1890, and the period is shown with a colored horizontal band. In 1849, ships sailed to Panama where passengers continued their travels across the isthmus by donkey. A change of color and symbol on that band indicates the opening of the locks of the Panama Canal in 1914. Symbols are identified at the beginning of the time line.

Near the bottom line a dot indicates the year in which each quilt was made; or, where its date has been estimated, the median date is used. If a quilt was made outside the state, the year of arrival in California is shown. Those made in California are identified with a poppy.

This time line offers in visual form much statistical information about the quilts within their historical perspective.

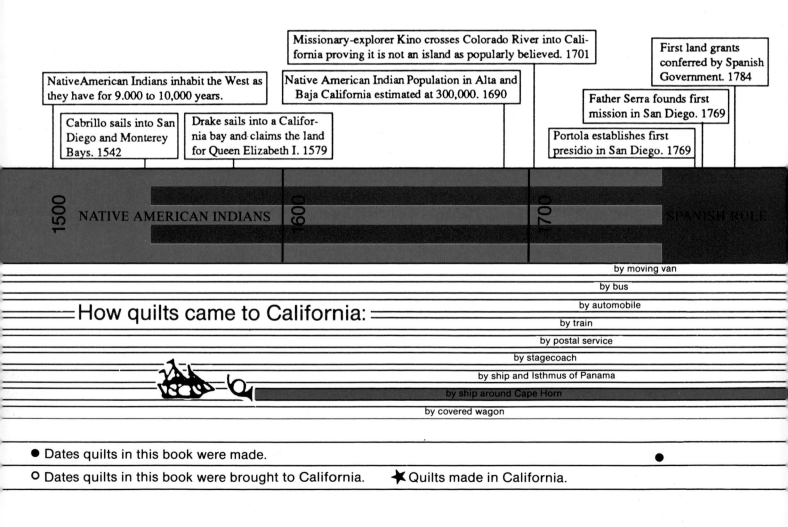

Native American Indians inhabit the West as they have for 9.000 to 10,000 years.

Cabrillo sails into San Diego and Monterey Bays. 1542

Drake sails into a California bay and claims the land for Queen Elizabeth I. 1579

Missionary-explorer Kino crosses Colorado River into California proving it is not an island as popularly believed. 1701

Native American Indian Population in Alta and Baja California estimated at 300,000. 1690

First land grants conferred by Spanish Government. 1784

Father Serra founds first mission in San Diego. 1769

Portola establishes first presidio in San Diego. 1769

1500 NATIVE AMERICAN INDIANS 1600 1700 SPANISH RULE

How quilts came to California:

by moving van
by bus
by automobile
by train
by postal service
by stagecoach
by ship and Isthmus of Panama
by ship around Cape Horn
by covered wagon

● Dates quilts in this book were made.

O Dates quilts in this book were brought to California.   ★ Quilts made in California.

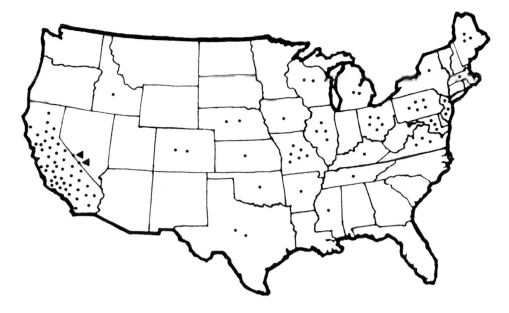

U.S. MAP: Each dot indicates a quilt's state of origin, including one from Hawaii and one from the province of Ontario, Canada. Two quilts were made en route to California, and they are shown by dots with arrows on the state's border.

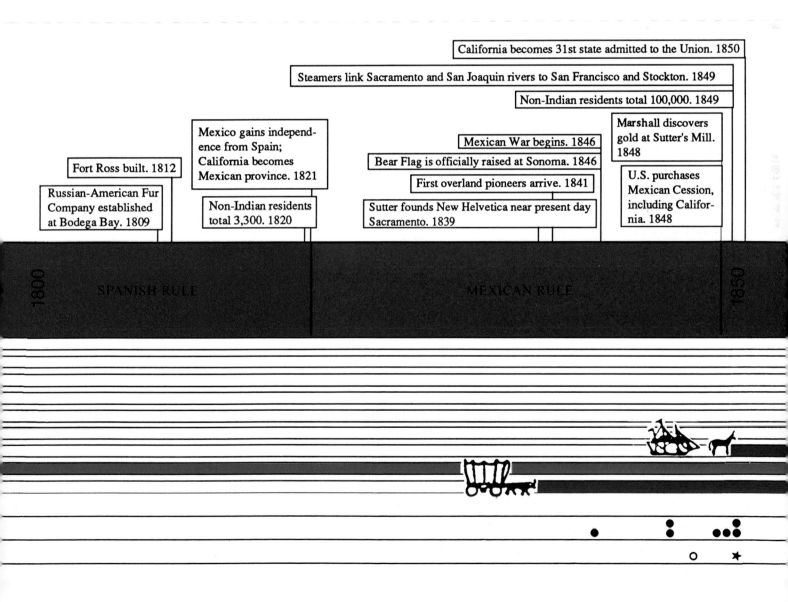

California becomes 31st state admitted to the Union. 1850

Steamers link Sacramento and San Joaquin rivers to San Francisco and Stockton. 1849

Non-Indian residents total 100,000. 1849

Mexico gains independence from Spain; California becomes Mexican province. 1821

Marshall discovers gold at Sutter's Mill. 1848

Mexican War begins. 1846

Fort Ross built. 1812

Bear Flag is officially raised at Sonoma. 1846

Russian-American Fur Company established at Bodega Bay. 1809

First overland pioneers arrive. 1841

U.S. purchases Mexican Cession, including California. 1848

Non-Indian residents total 3,300. 1820

Sutter founds New Helvetica near present day Sacramento. 1839

1800

SPANISH RULE

MEXICAN RULE

1850

Symbols beneath each color plate show at a glance information about the quilts. A poppy indicates that the quilt was made in California. For the out-of-state quilts, the means of transport to California is indicated. The symbols include:

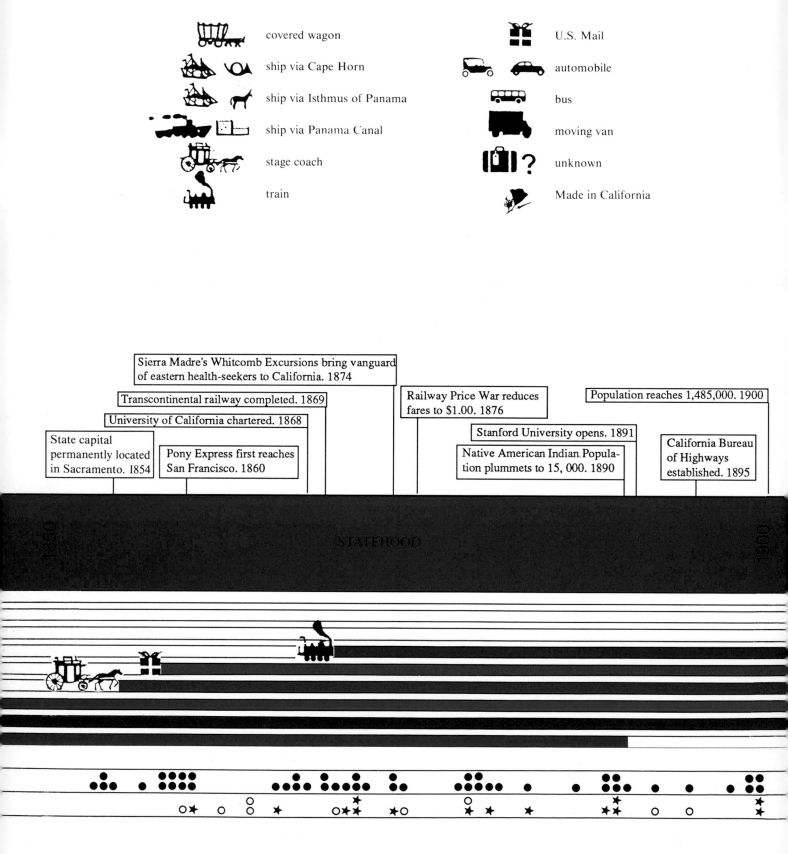

covered wagon

ship via Cape Horn

ship via Isthmus of Panama

ship via Panama Canal

stage coach

train

U.S. Mail

automobile

bus

moving van

unknown

Made in California

Sierra Madre's Whitcomb Excursions bring vanguard of eastern health-seekers to California. 1874

Transcontinental railway completed. 1869

Railway Price War reduces fares to $1.00. 1876

Population reaches 1,485,000. 1900

University of California chartered. 1868

Stanford University opens. 1891

State capital permanently located in Sacramento. 1854

Pony Express first reaches San Francisco. 1860

Native American Indian Population plummets to 15,000. 1890

California Bureau of Highways established. 1895

1850

STATEHOOD

1900

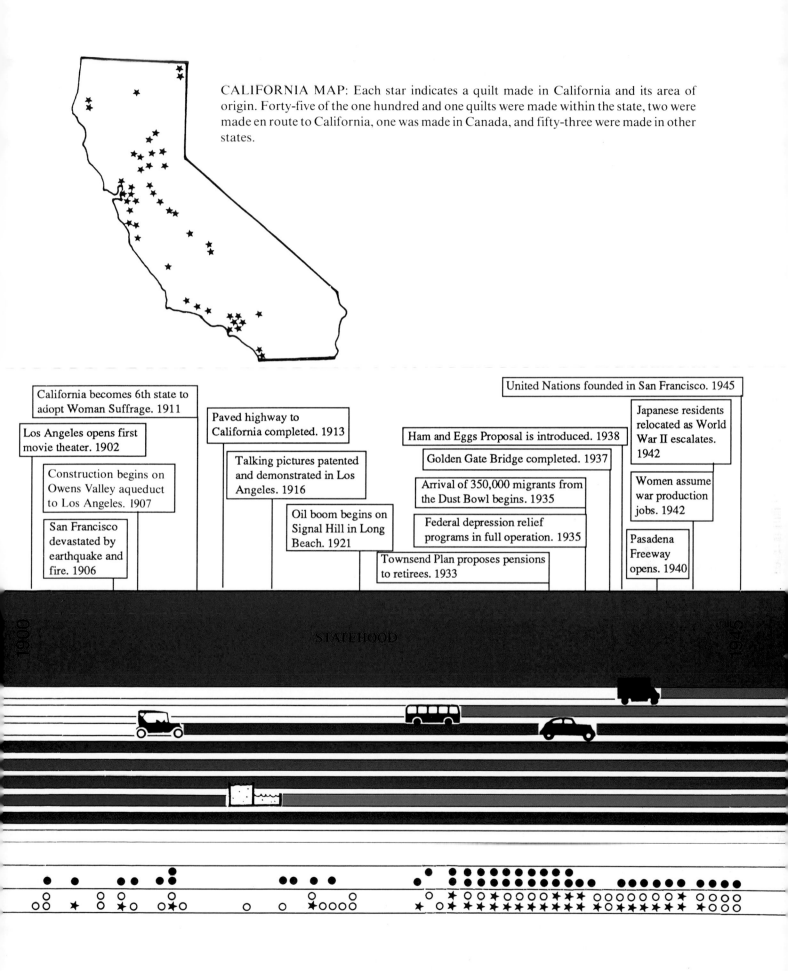

CALIFORNIA MAP: Each star indicates a quilt made in California and its area of origin. Forty-five of the one hundred and one quilts were made within the state, two were made en route to California, one was made in Canada, and fifty-three were made in other states.

California becomes 6th state to adopt Woman Suffrage. 1911

Los Angeles opens first movie theater. 1902

Construction begins on Owens Valley aqueduct to Los Angeles. 1907

San Francisco devastated by earthquake and fire. 1906

Paved highway to California completed. 1913

Talking pictures patented and demonstrated in Los Angeles. 1916

Oil boom begins on Signal Hill in Long Beach. 1921

United Nations founded in San Francisco. 1945

Japanese residents relocated as World War II escalates. 1942

Ham and Eggs Proposal is introduced. 1938

Golden Gate Bridge completed. 1937

Arrival of 350,000 migrants from the Dust Bowl begins. 1935

Federal depression relief programs in full operation. 1935

Townsend Plan proposes pensions to retirees. 1933

Women assume war production jobs. 1942

Pasadena Freeway opens. 1940

1900

STATEHOOD

1945

Quilt Dating

Each quilt in this book was examined by an expert at one of the Quilt Search Days, and an estimate of its age was given. There was an additional evaluation later by a panel of quilt historians. These two estimates, coupled with other known details relating to the quilt and its maker (dates of marriages, births, moves, etc.), provided the bracket dates. A quilt dated from 1870 to 1880, for example, would be placed in the same position chronologically as one dated 1860 to 1890, as each has a median date of 1875. A single year listed with a quilt indicates that specific evidence or documentation of its age determined the date given.

When a quilt was made at one time and quilted or finished later, the earlier date indicates the time when the top was produced, placing the work in its most appropriate period in terms of fabrics and style. A second date indicates the quilting or completion of that quilt.

Ho for California
That's the land for me.
I'm off to Sacramento
*With my dishpan on my knee.**

Blue Resist

The Brewster Quilt, dating from the eighteenth century, is unquestionably the oldest, and among the most unusual, of the quilts unfolded during Quilt Search Days. Blue-resist fabric embodies several unsolved mysteries of American textile history: where these blue-and-white fabrics were made, who made them, and what process was used in their production.

The lack of agreement over origin and method is epitomized in an article written some years ago about a blue-resist fabric pictured on the cover of *Antiques* magazine: "By various authorities in and out of sundry museums . . . [he] has learned that the piece was made in New Jersey, in Java, on the continent of Europe and in Japan. Its date has been set at from 1650 to 1900."[1]

Only the source of the rich blues is undisputed. It is indigo, the Spanish word for India, where the dye has been used for hundreds of years. A profitable American export, indigo was grown in the Colonies from 1740 on, the only blue dyestuff in the world until aniline (or coal-tar) dyes were discovered in 1856 (although indigo was not replaced until 1880). The processes involved in indigo dyeing are very complex.

Colonial fabrics were produced primarily through mordant-dyeing, in which a design was imprinted on fabric with a mordant, and dried. Only the mordanted areas then accepted the dye. Since indigo will *not* work with a mordant, some resist method was required to produce a pattern with this dye.

Blue resists are very distinctive, but compared with many delicate and carefully drawn European prints, they may seem naïve or primitive. Their appeal is in the directness and boldness of the designs, as well as in the brilliance and depth of the indigo. Although the patterns are sometimes printed in a single blue, they are more often printed in light and dark blue, as they are in the Brewster Quilt.

No records found offer any certainty as to when these fabric prints were made. Terminology adds to the confusion, for the term *blue resist* appears neither in shipping cargo lists nor in the records of printers or dyers, suggesting that the term was not then in use. In *America's Indigo Blues*, Florence Pettit quotes some early references:

> "blew callicoes," linens printed in "pail blue," and "blew pencilled calicoes," and in 1760 one John Hickey of Boston advertised that he "prints Linnens with true Blues and Whites." A year later the *Boston News Letter* announced that Mrs. John Haugin "stamps linen China blue and deep blue."[2]

Whether or not these refer to blue resist is uncertain and arguable. The enigma of provenance reveals the most divergent opinions among textile authorities.

Pettit cites several reasons for her belief that blue resist is American in origin; among them: (1) No examples or records are known in other countries (they have not been found in England, France, Germany, India, Indonesia, or China); and (2) Colonial newspapers contain advertisements, like Mrs. Haugin's, which could refer

* This is the verse sung during the gold rush and from which the title of our book is derived. (Sung to "Oh, Suzanna.")

Blue Resist quilt, family name: The Brewster Quilt, 1725–1800, came from Massachusetts (originally New York). 88″ x 96″. Quiltmaker unknown. Collection of Marjorie Miller Schultz.

Star of Bethlehem with Broderie Perse, 1830–1850, made in Virginia. 100″ x 100″. Quiltmaker unknown. Detail included. Collection of Katherine M. Cashman.

to blue-resist prints. All known examples originate in the Hudson River valley. Whether or not that is the origin is unproven.

Blue resists have two unique characteristics: "reserved ground" and "picotage dots," which is the pattern of whites within the blue areas. Reserved ground results from the use of a resist over the background area of the design. One theory as to how they were produced is offered by Florence Pettit in *America's Printed and Painted Fabrics*.[3] A stencil or template of the design (for example, a flower and stem) was placed on the fabric and traced (or pounced), moved and traced again, until the drawing was complete. Then the background was painted with resist, possibly by brush. It is believed that a paste resist was used, rather than a wax resist, which leaves the crackle lines characteristic of Javanese batik. The picotage dots may have been added by wood or copper blocks, which transferred a delicate pattern of paste onto the untreated area of the fabric; thus, the dots would appear as white when the fabric was dyed. Once the resist was applied and dried, the fabric could be dipped into the indigo vat. The wet fabric was then exposed to air, which allowed the indigo color to develop. If a second, darker blue was desired, parts of the first blue could be covered with resist and the whole piece redyed. Finally, the resist was removed and the patterned fabric emerged. Pettit lists various paste resist recipes that have been found, all including variations of such ingredients as pipe clay, wax, tallow, vitriol, gum arabic, and turpentine. A few recipes include brandy, egg-white, or calf-gall.

The theory of the hand-painted background accounts for variations among the design units. Easily noted in this quilt are variations in the light blue areas from one pattern unit to the next, suggesting that the second resist may have been painted freehand. The technique of painting cloth with wax had been used in India for centuries and was described in a letter written to an American in 1742, so the technique, while not identical, could have been known in America.

With possibly as few as one hundred known examples of blue resist extant in the country, primarily in museum collections, the Brewster Quilt is a rarity. It consists of two thirty-five-inch panels and one seventeen-inch panel. Part of the back appears to be newer than the rest of the quilt, perhaps dating from 1830 or 1840. The binding is in a print different from the panels, although the colors are identical. It is quilted in close parallel lines, resulting in a stipple effect.

The design motif of the Brewster Quilt is identical to major portions of a textile owned by The Henry Francis du Pont Winterthur Museum in Delaware, which is illustrated in both *Printed Textiles*[4] and *America's Indigo Blues*.[5] In the Winterthur piece, the vertical designs or columns are spaced farther apart, and additional designs of pheasant and deer are inserted. In the Brewster Quilt, a heavier overall effect is achieved through the proximity of the columns.

Because the blue-resist fabric is estimated to have been made in the 1700s and no evidence confirms an earlier time, the family's belief that it was made in the middle 1600s cannot be verified. However, the story is interesting, and the family history itself dates back to Elder Brewster's arrival on the *Mayflower* in 1620. At fifty-three, the oldest and probably the best educated of the ship's passengers fleeing religious persecution, Brewster traveled with his wife and two of their five children, Love and Wrestling. Jonathan followed in 1621, and Patience and Fear arrived on the *Anne* in 1623. Family accounts suggest that the quilt was made by Patience or Fear, although textile dating make it appear more likely that a descendant produced and quilted the piece. Both Patience (married to the fourth governor of Plymouth) and Fear (married to one of the *Mayflower* passengers) died in 1634. Patience left four or five small children.

Although the quilter's identity had been lost, the quilt itself fortunately remained in the family and was subsequently inherited by Thomas Brewster Palmer, born in 1843, who had moved from his birth state of New York to Kansas, where he was a minister. While serving in the Civil War, he contracted lung problems; these persisted and it was felt that a change of climate would be beneficial. The

Floral Sampler, 1840–1850, made in Virginia. 54″ x 83″. Quiltmaker: Anna Elizabeth Hinchkliff (1809–1864). Detail included. Collection of Suzanne Sampson.

Reverend Palmer traveled to California about 1876 by train, and brought the quilt with him. He then gave it to his daughter, who in turn passed it to *her* daughter, who is the present owner.

Star of Bethlehem

The finely sewn Broderie Perse and the vitality of sawtooth edges tell us much about this quiltmaker's skills and artistry. But they do not tell us who she was. The grandfather of the quilt's present owner came to San Francisco after serving in the Civil War, believing that the California climate would be beneficial to his health. He wrote to the famous newspaper publisher William Randolph Hearst, who hired the young attorney to work at his office in San Luis Obispo and at the cattle ranch on the coast. He later returned to the East Coast, married, and brought his bride to California.

Among their children was Katherine R. Venable, born in 1870. Fifty-nine years later, Katherine took the train from Berkeley to Hampton-Sydney, Virginia, to reestablish family ties, and returned to California with several quilts.

One of those quilts is this Star of Bethlehem, which has appliquéd chintz motifs, each surrounded by a green-print sawtooth border and filled with hanging-diamond quilting. A larger pattern of quilted diamonds covers the star. Inherited in 1975 by Katherine's niece, the quilt is known only to have been made by "someone in the family."

Floral Sampler

Every quilter has heard at least one story of a quilt being snipped down the middle as Mother settles a never-ending dispute with this drastic action. Here is further evidence that passions can run high over the ownership of a quilt.

Anna Elizabeth Hinchkliff lived in Virginia, having come to America from Hernshaw, England, where she was born in 1809. It was in Virginia that she made this delicate and charming appliquéd quilt. How many children she had is not known, but she did have a daughter, Olive, to whom this quilt was given.

Olive and her husband, the Reverend Enoch B. Dolly, moved with their four children to Parkville, Missouri, taking the quilt with them. Enoch was a self-taught preacher and knowledgeable about raising cane for molasses, so he was hired to join the staff at Park College, where he taught Bible and farming.

Olive died in Missouri, an area that in the middle 1800s was synonymous with pneumonia, rheumatism, and colds. Cabins were damp, winters hard, and frontier doctors scarce. The exact cause of Olive's death at fifty-five is not known, but she left three daughters and a son. Enoch later remarried.

Apparently, the quilt was much appreciated and highly prized by the family. Two of Olive's daughters, Hattie Belle and Burr Mattie (granddaughters of Anna), "fussed about the ownership" until Burr resolved the issue with precision and finality by cutting the quilt in two. The scissors-wielding sibling then sent one half of the quilt to her sister, Hattie Belle, in 1912. Hattie bound the cut edge and used it on the bed of her eighth daughter, after which it was stored for years before being mailed to Anna's great-great-granddaughter in California. The whereabouts of the other half is unknown.

In the finely quilted background, grapes and leaves are firmly stuffed to create a rich relief pattern. Only the butterflies are buttonhole stitched, in contrast to the blind stitch used elsewhere. A final flourish is the elaborate meandering border that gracefully maneuvers the corners and reflects the colors of the appliqué blocks.

Baltimore Album Quilt, 1848, made in Maryland. 106″ x 91″. Quiltmakers: Mary A. Ellis, Amelia Magee, Mary Harrington, Marion G. McCormick, Mrs. E. Eugenia Murphy, M. L. Pendergast, Caroline M. Sheppard, and Sarah R. M. Slicer. Detail included. Private collection. 📷?

Born William Watson in 1808, he was admitted to the county bar at twenty-one, and at twenty-eight was elected to the city council. In 1838 he represented his city in the House of Delegates and was its speaker in 1843. Just three years later he was selected to command the battalion that was to join General Zachary Taylor's army in Mexico. After being commissioned a colonel, he led his battalion on a march of three hundred miles to Monterey. There, Colonel Watson was struck while leading a charge. A bullet severed his jugular vein, and he died five minutes later, in the arms of Lieutenant Oden Bowie. He was thirty-eight.

> Colonel Watson's personality, as well as his courage and capacity as a soldier, had greatly endeared him not only to the men under his command, but equally to the rest of the army in Mexico and to the public in his native state, and the news of his death caused more than the usual regret attendant upon the casualties in war.[7]

The popularity of the unmarried colonel is attested to by at least two quilts known to have been made in his memory. This is one. The other, an equally remarkable Album quilt, is in the Shelburne Museum in Shelburne, Vermont. Additionally, the Baltimore Museum of Art has in its collection an Album quilt made for a Methodist minister in 1847, which includes a block depicting an urn on which Watson's name is appliquéd in red.

Colonel Watson's political and business life, his association with the Columbian Fire Department and with the International Order of Odd Fellows, and his captaincy of a militia company known as the Independent Blues all contributed to his distinctive reputation and popularity. The signature of a Thomas Bennet, christened in 1801 and therefore a few years older than Colonel Watson, appears enigmatically on the memorial block of this quilt.

Who planned or organized the making of this quilt is unknown, but eight women contributed to it. Their names are executed in calligraphy and embroidery on the quilt. The stuffed, flowing Feather in the border, the hundreds of Flying Geese, and the quality of both appliqué and quilting attest to the superlative skills of these needlewomen, as well as to the high regard in which the memory of Colonel Watson was held.

How the quilt came to California is puzzling, and no known record exists to indicate who might have brought it. However, around 1937 it was found folded in a trunk in a garage and was included in a garage sale. According to the present owner, it was:

> purchased for five dollars. The purchaser proceeded to put it in her washer to clean it. She then enthusiastically showed her treasure to Faith Phillips, an Altadena resident. Faith Phillips, knowing of my interest in quiltmaking, invited me over to see this wonderful quilt. A few years later...the purchaser...gifted the quilt to her friend, Faith, who cherished it for many years....Ten years ago...a conservator was appointed to handle her affairs. It became necessary for the quilt to be sold. The conservator called in a dealer who specialized in quilts and asked her to take it on consignment. I saw it on display in her booth at an antiques show and immediately bought it. It has been in my possession for approximately ten years.[8]

Memorial Album

In 1849 or 1850, the widow of the Reverend Jacob Geiger was presented with an appliquéd Album quilt top. It was made in her husband's honor, as he had remained the pastor of his church for thirty-one years, from 1817 through 1848. Upon Reverend Geiger's death, the women of the Congregation of Manchester

Memorial Album Quilt, 1849, made in Maryland. 108″ x 106″. Quiltmakers: Ladies of the Congregation of the Manchester German Reform Church. Collection of Marjorie E. Wood.

The Machado Quilt, c. 1850, made in California. 62½″ x 82″. Quiltmaker: Dona Juana de Dios Machado Alipás Wrightington (Ridington) (1810–1901). Collection of the San Diego Historical Society.

German Reform Church of Manchester, Maryland, did this remarkable work in his memory.

Born in 1793, Jacob was one of six children left fatherless with a mother who struggled for her family's survival. Originally urged into tailoring, he later received religious training (against his mother's wishes).[9]

A vigorous man in both body and spirit, he traveled to eight communities to preach, baptize, marry, and bury. Later he spent several years in Philadelphia studying homeopathic medicine, so that he could treat the ill as he traveled in his work. His first wife bore him seven children before she died at age thirty-four. He married again and had three more sons. Two of his children died as babies, and two in their early adulthood.

Riding from church to church on horseback, Reverend Geiger carried his manuscripts in one saddlebag and his homeopathic medicines in the other. He was "endowed with…wondrous elements of endurance,"[10] and his popularity was attested to by the several thousands who attended the fifty-five-year-old minister's funeral.

In the quilt's center and most somber block, his tomb is depicted, giving his death date, 1849. In other blocks of fine blind-stitch appliqué, Broderie Perse, buttonhole stitch, stuffed work, and reverse-appliqué are ink-inscribed Bible verses and the names of the women who made the blocks. A swag border, which also contains signatures and intricate designs, attests to the fine needlework skills of these devoted friends.

After its presentation to Reverend Geiger's widow, the quilt top passed through four generations, from mother to daughter or aunt to niece, and remains unquilted.

In 1942, the great-great-granddaughter of Reverend Geiger left Philadelphia to join her husband, who was working with naval intelligence at Treasure Island in San Francisco. She came to California on a troop train; the quilt top arrived later, in the moving van.

Machado Appliqué

A morning ceremony, followed by breakfast and dancing until an afternoon dinner at two, and then a full night of dancing heralded the marriage of Juana de Dios Machado to Dámasio Alipáz (Alipás), whose father and grandfather were well-known soldiers. Juana was fifteen when she married, and she states that her marriage was in 1825; thus, her birth year was 1810 (another source places her marriage in 1829, and her birth in 1814). The three daughters of this marriage all grew to adulthood. María Arcadia, the second daughter, married Captain Robert D. Israel, for years the lighthouse keeper at Point Loma. Josefa, the third, married Juan Peters. In 1878, Thomas C. Savage recorded these oral interviews as an agent for Hubert H. Bancroft. The original recollections dictated by Juana remain in the Bancroft Library in Berkeley, California.

Juana was about sixty-four at the time of the interviews, and she recalled in vivid detail her life in the San Diego Presidio. She was one of the nine children of María Serafina Valdéz, wife of José Manuel Machado, the grantee of the twenty-six-thousand-acre Rancho Las Virgenes.

Dámasio Alipáz (Alipás), was killed around 1835 in Sonora, and approximately five years later, Juana married Thomas Wrightington (Ridington), from Fall River, Massachusetts, who is well represented in San Diego history. Juana and Thomas had two sons, José and Luis, and a daughter, Serafina.

Juana Machado Wrightington seated outside her adobe house in Old Town (San Diego). c. 1892. Courtesy the San Diego Historical Society, Ticor Collection.

> After Father Antonio Ubach came to San Diego in 1866, he often asked Juana to act as midwife, to help with sick ones and to act as interpreter. She never hesitated and later on was foster mother to several children.…It is said that Juana was the first woman of Spanish descent to speak the English language in Old Town and that she conversed in

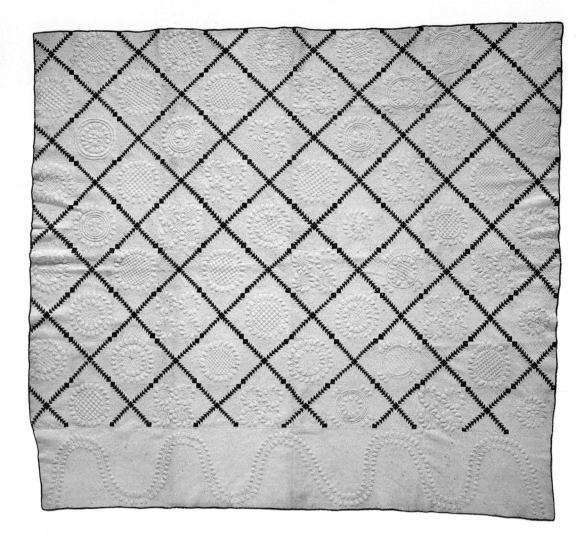

Wild Goose Chase with Stuffed
Work, 1840–1860, made in Ohio.
88″ x 97″. Quiltmakers: Margaret
Glenn Wiley (1807–1882) and
Nancy Glenn Wiley Mosgrove
(1830–1902). Detail included. Col-
lection of the Fresno City and
County Historical Society (The
Mosgrove Collection).

English, Spanish and the provincial speech of the Indians with equal fluency.[11]

Juana's story in the Bancroft Library is filled with details of life at the presidio and mission in San Diego. She was present "when the Spanish flag was lowered and the Mexican raised"[12] in 1822, and lived there when California became a state in 1850.

It was from Doña Lugarda, the wife of a lieutenant in the Active Militia Squadron of Mazatlán, that she learned sewing. Juana states that her mentor was "very skillful in all kinds of sewing, artificial flowers and other fancy work."[13]

Juana Machado, her mother, and many other women found that the frequent changes in government and policies had an adverse effect on their fortunes.

> Many owners of property had no written deeds; and they had been told by men, whose words they accepted without question, that they would never be molested and felt that their words were all the evidence needed. When the United States land agents confiscated properties, Juana lost many of the things she had inherited and worked hard for.[14]

Seeking to reform American (English) common law, which protected male rights, the new state of California adopted the Spanish civil law, which protected family rights. Additional reforms, however, eroded those rights:

> By the end of the century, California women had no more rights than did women in most of the eastern states. Not until after California women obtained the vote in 1911 were married women able to regain their property rights. While these laws affected all California women, they had a disproportionately harsh effect on some Hispanic women who were attempting to preserve property for their children.[15]

Juana's quilt is estimated by the San Diego Historical Society to have been made around 1850, when she was in her forties and living in or near Old Town in San Diego. Where Juana learned this work or what she saw to inspire her is unknown, and no other quilts of hers are known to have survived. Her quilt top seems scarcely able to contain so much exuberance, vitality, and energy. The two red fabrics are whipstitch appliquéd to the white cotton top, as is a running vine border. The batting is cotton.

Everett W. Israel, a descendant of Juana's, presented the quilt to the San Diego Historical Society in 1953.

Juana Machado Wrightington surrounded by the cactus hedge in Old Town (San Diego). c. 1893. Courtesy the San Diego Historical Society, Ticor Collection.

Juana Machado Wrightington, age 83. c. 1893. Courtesy the San Diego Historical Society, Ticor Collection.

Wild Goose Chase

Stitched among the colorful alphabets and numbers on a linen sampler are pine trees, flowers, a rooster, and these words: "Margaret Glenn, born in Mason County, Kentucky in 1807."

After her marriage to William Wiley, Margaret moved from Kentucky to Urbana, Ohio, where Nancy Glenn, one of their two children, was born in 1830. It was probably in Urbana that this fine quilt was made. The family believes that the collection of quilts that has passed down through five or six generations was made by Margaret and her daughter, Nancy, perhaps jointly.

Nancy married William Foster Mosgrove, a medical doctor, in 1849, and spent her lifetime in Ohio, where she raised three children.

When the old family home in Urbana was closed, many of the furnishings were stored for years in a warehouse. Some of the family quilts were brought to California in 1900, but this one came by car in 1930, along with what would form a museum collection of clothing and other household pieces. The quilt was brought by the grandparents of the most recent owner.

The stuffed work and stipple quilting create a beautiful relief pattern where

This portrait, c. 1885, of Nancy Glen Mosgrove was photographed from a hand-painted porcelain plate. The dress she is wearing, as well as her Wild Goose Chase quilt, form part of a museum collection at the Fresno City and County Historical Society.

Describing their 1873 Christmas dinner, Anna wrote that she served roast turkey, cranberry sauce, mashed potatoes, tomatoes, pickles and celery, bread, butter, preserved apples, mince and squash pies, pound cake, cheese, cold water, tea, pears, and grapes. She added, "Mr. T. helped prepare most everything and clean up afterwards."[22]

Anna was doing sewing at home, specializing in buttonholes and cuffs (corded and tucked). When the baby had scarlet fever, Anna wrote, "In slang phrase...am about played out....I have never been so low in flesh."[23] She commented to her mother that the medicine she had taken since the birth of her child was her "best ever" and seemed to control her ongoing headaches. Still, she found it hard to care for the baby and keep up with the house, with never a chance to sit down.

In January 1883, Anna wrote, "The last day of December 1882 will long be remembered in California as we were treated to a real old-fashioned down-East snow storm the like of which was never known about San Francisco before. There was much sport, hastily made sleighs and snowballing. Some people were foolish enough to lose their tempers."[24]

Anna's letters home revealed that the coming year did not promise to be better than the last nine. She found little buttonhole business, and felt prematurely aged and wrinkled.

When Anna died in Oakland, after twenty-five years of marriage, the quilt was left to her only child, Eugene. Sallie Wade, a friend of Anna's, wrote a letter of sympathy to Eugene in which she stated, "A keepsake mentioned by Mrs. Thurston for me...I should prize anything that was hallowed by her possession and use, and whatever you may reserve for me will be above nice. A work basket or something that she *used* or *made* will be treasured most."[25]

Anna's parents, her grandfather, other relatives, and friends in Maine had all contributed to this Nine-Patch Variation, which now belongs to the maker's grand-daughter.

Tulip Tree

Eliza Warren Brown was born in Ohio in 1817. After her marriage she lived in Mercer County, Illinois, where seven of her ten children survived to adulthood.

Mary Twist, Eliza's granddaughter, compiled a family history, *Just an Ordinary Family*, which offers information about the Warrens.

Mary Twist uses her quilt, conveniently stretched on its frame, as a desk on which to compile her family history. Mary is the granddaughter of quiltmaker Eliza Brown.

> Mary Ann...[Eliza's] eldest daughter...always loved outdoor work but hated taking care of the numerous babies, as they happened along from time to time, while Elmira, 16 months younger than she, loved caring for the little ones, but hated the field work. By the cruel irony of fate, when the sisters grew up and married, Mary Ann had nine children while Aunt El had but two, nature's little joke.[26]

The book's recollections also include the following passage:

> The youngest in the family—[was] Aunt Thursta. She was born with a hunchback and other deformities, but had the loveliest, most unselfish personality of anyone I ever knew. After the rest of the boys and girls were grown she supported herself and my grandmother [Eliza] by sewing.[27]

Eliza and her daughter Thursta were both buried in Los Angeles, although it is not known when they left Illinois, where the weather was "alternate rain and snow, with a great deal of slush and mud."[28] Eliza died in 1889, and Thursta was killed when struck by an automobile while alighting from a streetcar in 1925.

Whereas little of a personal nature is known about the quiltmaker, we do know that she had a lively, spirited approach to her work. The bold strength, the sure use of design and color, and the beautiful relief patterns of the quilting tell us much about her. This was not her only quilt and, judging by the needlework, not her first.

At least one other quilt is still owned by her descendants. This one belongs to Eliza's great-great-granddaughter.

Barrister's Block

Through six generations, this Barrister's Block quilt has passed from mother to daughter or granddaughter. The present owner says, "It was my Mother's most beloved heirloom. Like an unbroken line of quilting stitches, it symbolizes for me my maternal heritage."[29]

In 1815 in Chili (now Rochester), New York, Sarah F. Paull was born into a family that "held high positions in New York."[30] She married Alexander Cameron, who was by turns a carpenter, a real estate entrepreneur, a Michigan State legislator, and a '49er.

Besides being the first schoolteacher in Barry County, Michigan, Sarah raised five children. She was thirty-five and living in Kalamazoo when her husband left to pan for gold in Placerville, California. A quilt begun in his absence was given to her daughter, Jeanette E. Cameron, who was eleven when her father departed. A letter written by Jeanette in 1902 gives her recollection of the circumstances:

> *1902 A Merry Christmas and a Happy New Year to each one of you Dear Ones! Grand-Ma Cameron pieced this quilt in 1850 and 51 while our Father was in California digging gold. He was one of the "forty-niners" who went overland and suffered innumerable hardships. A ship brought letters only once a month. What thoughts she must have stitched into these blue and white blocks while she waited for letters. This was on the frames for a week and there were five quilting parties. Oh, that I had the names of these forty ladies whose stitches are taken in it. They are all gone, the last one Mrs. Levi Krause died one year ago aged eighty-nine. What bountiful suppers they gathered around at early candle-light, taking their leave leisurely afterwards. The pattern for quilting was pasteboard cut in [the] shape of a "wheel" a "tulip" and some other flowers (?) the outlines of which were marked with lead pencil. It was "new" and considered very artistic. One afternoon March twelfth, eighteen hundred and fifty-two, when the quilt was nearly finished, my Father reached home. At the US Mint in Philadelphia he had exchanged his gold dust for new minted coins of gold. That evening he put up both table "leaves" and Pa emptied the buckskin bags that he had worn in a belt under his clothes. There was over four thousand dollars in immense fifty dollar pieces, "eagles," tens and fives. I was twelve years old and the sight of this quilt brings these scenes to mind. My Mother associated it with the thought of the friends who quilted it.*
>
>

Mother Ayres
December 25th 1902[31]

Diagonal quilting contrasts with a flower pattern (or tulip wheel) in each white triangle of this quilt. The great-granddaughter of the quiltmaker brought the quilt to California by train after one of her many visits to the East. She later passed the quilt to her granddaughter.

Appliquéd Flower

A 1940 sale in Tomkinsville, Kentucky, offered Effa White's personal property to buyers. Included among her personal effects was a quilt. "It seems the younger Whites didn't care too much for antiques and some of them said later they had forgotten the history of the quilt."[32]

Effa was unmarried, and the estate sale may have been held to dispose of her

Original Flower Appliqué, 1850–
1860, made in Kentucky. 81″ x
95″. Quiltmaker unknown. Detail
included. Collection of Betty
Bushong.

parents' belongings. Knowing that the quilt would be sold, the present owner's mother-in-law made a special point of being at the sale. While it was the quilt she specifically wanted, she bought a "bundle" of things with which it was sold. The exact price paid is not known, but because she didn't *have* much money, the family is certain it wasn't much, perhaps five dollars.

Hetti S. Bushong, who attended the auction, was alerted to the quilt's existence since her family was distantly related to the Whites. The story, as she was able to put it together, is as follows:

> [The quilt] was made by the descendants of Thomas White, Sr., the Revolutionary War orderly of Gen. Francis Marion who served General Marion and his official visitor, a British officer, the famous meal of baked potatoes on a slab of bark.
>
> The story of General Marion's orderly was told in the old Goodrich Fifth Reader. When General Marion was at Georgetown, S.C., a British officer came to his camp to arrange the transfer of prisoners. General Marion invited him to stay for dinner, then bade his orderly serve the meal.
>
> Private White placed a slab of bark between them, on the log on which the officers were sitting. The bark was loaded with baked potatoes, which the soldier had just raked from the hot ashes of a camp fire.
>
> "Surely, General, this is not your ordinary fare?" asked the British officer.
>
> "Indeed it is," replied General Marion, "but having today the honor of your company, we are so happy to have more than our usual allowance."
>
> During the Civil War, the quilt belonged to the Whites' grandson. The family hid it in Walden cave, two and a half miles from Tompkinsville, when the Bragg's army marched through here in 1862. It is a quilt of great beauty and unusual pattern. The lining was home-spun and hand-woven.[33]

The design is original and the white-embroidered flowers over the printed ground are unique. Brown stems and leaves are believed to have been hand-dyed with walnut. In the appliqué blocks, quilting stitches echo flowers and leaves, meandering in curved lines throughout in contrast to the diagonal quilting of the beige blocks.

Whether the quiltmaker was Thomas White's daughter, a daughter-in-law, or some other relative remains a mystery. The quilt remained in the White family until the estate sale in 1940, and was then given by the collector to her daughter-in-law in California.

Whig Rose

Quilts were often shared ventures, on which sisters or mothers and daughters combined energies and talents. Occasionally, the work continued over several generations, coming out of drawers or trunks years after being started. Work on a top, interrupted by a move or a death, might be completed by a descendant who added quilting.

This Whig Rose was one such venture, started by Lavena Ellen Burgett, who was born in 1829 in Harpersfield, Ohio. She married Edmond Tift Schellenger, a blacksmith, and bore him two children. It was shortly after the birth of her second child, Clara, that Lavena died at age thirty.

Lavena's older sister, Almena Isabell Burgett, cared for the two small motherless children. Almena married Edmond some time later, and they had two more children. It was Almena who finished her sister's handsome Whig Rose quilt.

The different greens that are used in the quilt resulted from changes in the available fabric. Family history says that the quilt was started before the Civil War, and since it is believed originally to be Lavena's work, certainly before 1859. It was finished later, so dye lots of the fabrics varied.

Almena Isabell Burgett is shown in this daguerreotype, c. 1865, with her nephew and niece (who are also her stepchildren), Clarence Hector and Clara Louise Schellenger.

Whig Rose, 1850–1865, made in
Illinois. 82″ x 81″. Quiltmakers:
Lavena Ellen Burgett (1829–1859)
and Almena Isabell Burgett (1827–
1910). Detail included. Collection
of Edwina Allen Atterbury.

In 1871, just two years after the Union Pacific (going west) met the Central Pacific (going east) and made transcontinental train travel a reality, the Schellengers migrated from Capron, Illinois, where the quilt was made, to California. "Adelbert, who was four years old, remembered the train trip and often told how the train moved so slowly that they got off and gathered wood to burn in the iron stoves on the train."[34] The family settled in O'Banion Corners, Sutter County.

The present owner recalls the following:

> When my mother first saw this quilt she was told by my grandmother that if she ever had a daughter the quilt would be given to her. Lucky me, I was that daughter, and true to her word my grandmother willed the Whig Rose to me. I was the first girl in the Allen family for 75 years!...My grandmother told me she remembered sewing on the quilt with her stepmother, Almena, when she was a little girl. The quilt was displayed on her bed when she had company, mainly when she had "the girls" over for lunch.[35]

The fine quilting stitches and the mastery of both appliqué and reverse-appliqué distinguish this Whig Rose quilt, with its unique and exquisitely executed swag border. Only loving care can bring a white quilt through so many decades in mint condition.

Lavena's great-granddaughter now prizes this quilt, given to her by her grandmother in 1940.

Road to California

Mary Margaret Hezlep arrived in California in 1859 when she was fifteen years old, after traveling overland nearly seven months in a wagon train. She had been assembling blocks for her Road to California quilt all through a difficult and hazardous trip. With her on this trip were her mother, who was thirty-seven, and her maternal grandmother, who was seventy-two. They, along with aunts and friends, participated in the piecing as their wagons groaned and jolted their way west.

Melvina Shuey Hezlep (from a daguerreotype, c. 1850), worked with her mother and her daughter to make the Road to California quilt as they crossed the plains.

Inked onto the fabric are the names of over thirty members of their wagon train who came from Iowa, Illinois, and Ohio. "Ho for California" is written optimistically and beautifully on one block; others read "Left Hamilton, April 15, 1859," "Seven months on the road," "Crossed the Plains," and "Arrived in Columbia, Oct. 28, 1859." Pieces for the quilt were cut the preceding winter with the help of Mary's paternal grandmother, and aunt, and others in Illinois.

Mary's grandmother, Margaret Shuperd Shuey, who helped piece on the overland crossing, was the wife of General Martin Shuey, who was born in Pennsylvania in 1785. He had moved with his parents to Ohio in 1805, and there met his bride-to-be. He helped form a rifle company for protection from Indian raids and thus began a military career. He and Margaret married in 1808, after which he fought in the War of 1812 and, as a brigadier general, commanded Forts Brown, Laramie, and Winchester. Margaret gave birth to eleven children, four of whom died in infancy. In 1820, the Shueys moved with their children to Indiana. Martin resigned his military position in 1826 at age forty-two in order to have more time with his family. Three years later they moved again, this time to Illinois. There the family remained for thirty years before a final move.

John Shuey, Mary's uncle, made seven trips to California via Panama, and it was because of his enthusiasm and encouragement that his sister, Melvina Shuey Hezlep, her husband, James Hezlep, and their only child, Mary, joined Margaret and Martin Shuey on a wagon train heading for the West. When they arrived, they were met by John at the mouth of the Carson River.

Mary, who had so carefully assembled many of the Nine-Patch blocks, became

Margaret Shuperd Shuey made the covered-wagon crossing at age seventy-two with her husband, General Martin Shuey.

a teacher in California before her marriage. Over twenty years after her westward journey, Mary finished the quilt and gave it to her daughter, Mae Smallman, on her fourteenth birthday in 1884. This special gift recounted for Mae those seven months on the trail, a quilt stitched full of history in which Mae's mother, grandmother, and great-grandmother left evidence of their episodic adventure across the country.

The current owner is Mae Smallman French's granddaughter, the great-granddaughter of the young woman who made that incredible crossing at age fifteen.

Pomegranate

Paired hearts and clasped hands, symbols of love and marriage, are quilted resolutely, though delicately, into the background of this quilt. Firmly embedded between appliquéd pomegranates and paired eagles holding ribbons in their beaks is the quiltmaker's signature, "Mary E. Lynes, 1859." These quilted drawings, while soft and subtle, also express an unhesitating hand, a firmness of spirit, and an intrepid, faithful heart.

When Hannah Bruington Victor married James Madison Lynes and they left Kentucky to move west in the 1830s, Missouri's statehood was over ten years old and Boone County was a thriving area. It was there that Hannah, at fourteen, gave birth to Mary, the first of her thirteen children. James became a successful businessman and landowner.

At twenty-five, Mary was engaged to James Harrison White. Family history maintains that the size of the quilt (a generous 98 inches by 108 inches) resulted from Mary's promise to keep working on the quilt until the return of her sweetheart from the Civil War, so the stitched "1859" refers to an engagement date. The eagles and their messages relate convincingly to the young man's absence and the struggle for reunification of the country. Mary's concerns are comprehensive, encompassing both her personal life and her world. James served in the Union Army; he did return, and in 1861 they married.

The Whites settled in Columbia, Missouri, where James was a merchant. Mary gave birth to two daughters in 1862 and 1863, and to a son in 1866, just five months before her death. It is believed that this quilt, which she mentioned on her deathbed, was given into the keeping of one of her sisters to later pass on to Mary's daughter. This highly prized legacy was awarded a silver spoon at a Missouri State Fair.

The superlative workmanship of finely stitched appliqué and stuffed areas attests to the superior skills of this quiltmaker. Mary's younger sister, Laura E. Lynes, who was twelve at the time of Mary's death, may have been the one to whose care the quilt was entrusted. Laura, too, became an accomplished quilter. Depicted in *Missouri Heritage Quilts*, Laura's quilt incorporates pomegranates identical to Mary's, enlarged into a medallion design.[36] Similarities in the quilts' border vines, grapes, and flowers suggest that many of Mary's patterns were used in her sister's quilt. The clasped hands are repeated in several places (although Laura never married), and a church is drawn in fine quilted lines.

The owner of Laura's quilt describes the pattern used by the sisters to quilt the hand as a shape simply cut from a lined sheet of tablet paper. These delicate patterns survived through generations, but are now believed to be lost.

In 1930, upon the death of Mary's daughter, the quilt passed to her granddaughter to whom it had been promised. When the quilt left Missouri to come to California, Mary's grandfather was very upset; not just because someone would actually want to leave Missouri, but more because the quilt was being taken from its home. The current owner, a great-granddaughter of Mary E. Lynes, moved to California in the early 1940s when her husband attended the University of California, Berkeley. They brought the quilt with them by car.

Alice Lee Hourigan, at age sixty-seven, proudly displays the quilt made by her mother, Mary Elizabeth Lynes, in front of the old family home in New Franklin, Missouri, in 1930.

Northumberland Star

Sarah Ann Bowers, thirty, and Elijah Harelson, thirty-seven, married in Warren County, Kentucky, in 1837. Just a few days after their double-wedding ceremony with friends, the new bride and groom rode off on horseback to a farming life in Wisconsin. Sarah was riding her own pony, with a red velvet saddle and riding outfit given to her by her father.

A daughter, Isabel, and a son, William, was born to them. In 1859, when the children were grown, Elijah made his first trip to California. He determined then to move his family west, and in 1864 the Reynolds-Harelson-Graves train, consisting of sixty-eight wagons, left Grant County, Wisconsin, for the four-month trip to Calaveras County, California. Accompanying Elijah and Sarah Ann on their long trek west in the wagon train were William and Isabel. Isabel had married David Ramsey Reynolds in 1862, in Grant County. David, twenty-seven, had also been in California, having traveled in the 1853 Reynolds-Salmon train of forty wagons.[37]

It was on this 1864 trip, when heavy storms of rain, snow, or dust forced them to seek protection inside the wagon, that their barrel of homemade crackers provided meals. A family history includes this recollection:

> After the loss of three of Grandfather Reynolds's horses—from drinking alkali water, and grass very scarce—it was necessary to lighten the wagons, and the following was left by the roadside with Grandmother's tears: five good quilts, handmade; one feather bed; extra cooking utensils; a keg of syrup; one gun, broken up so the Indians couldn't use it; and one wagon with the sign on it "help yourself" in hopes the next train would get it.[38]

Family recollections of the trip, later compiled and published by Isabel's daughter, stated the following:

> Each of my grandmothers had one small leather trunk and a carpet bag....Among the special treats during the long summer of 1864 was a grand, green salad...cabbage bought from the Mormons in Salt Lake...and fresh peach pie, given to the train by the lady at the stage station at Carson City, Nevada...it was Mother's first peach pie and she said it was delicious.[39]

Family history also tells us that, upon their arrival in Big Tree Grove, a dance was held—it took place atop a single huge redwood stump.

In California, Elijah and Sarah Ann settled on the Stanislaus River in San Joaquin County, later moving with their son, William, to their ranch home on French Camp Road. Isabel and David settled on their land in East Union Corner.

A year before the move to California, Sarah Ann had made a last visit to her mother, Elizabeth Bowers, in Kentucky. Her mother said, "Sally, I know I'll never see you again, going on that long and dangerous trip to that far off land."[40] At that farewell, Elizabeth gave her daughter a treasured gift. Sarah Ann's paternal grandfather, William Bowers, a drum major in the Revolutionary War, had won two silver spoons in a musical competition. He was killed in the war without ever having seen his son William, to whom the spoons were given. When William married Elizabeth, he had four additional spoons made and engraved with the initials W. E. B. (for William and Elizabeth Bowers). In Sarah Ann's hands, the spoons survived the wagon trip,[41] as did quilts that Sarah Ann and Isabel had made together.

The hearts in the vine border of this Northumberland Star quilt suggest the possibility that it was made for Isabel's wedding. A quilted feather runs through the sashing, with diagonal and straight parallel lines throughout.

The present owner of this quilt received it from her great-aunt, who was a daughter of Isabel and the granddaughter of Sarah Ann.

Northumberland Star with Heart Border, 1850–1870, made in Wisconsin. 76″ x 81″. Quiltmakers: Sarah Ann Bowers Harelson (1807–1902) and Isabel Harelson Reynolds (1844–1923). Collection of Louise L. Lyons.

Friendship Star, 1850–1870, made in Maine. 76″ x 89″. Quiltmaker: Mary Elizabeth Simpson Sperry (1833–1921). Collection of Martha Sperry.

Friendship

In the 1860s, Mary Elizabeth Simpson traveled by ship around the Horn, then a journey of between one and three hundred days. She was born in 1833 to English parents in Brunswick, Maine, where she and her brothers grew up. It was to visit two of her brothers, Andrew M. Simpson and Robert W. Simpson, that she made her trip to California. Both were associated with the Simpson Lumber Company. Andrew, the company's vice president, resided in Stockton.

Mary brought with her on this trip a quilt, full of family signatures and dated 1860–1861. The center of each star highlights the penned name of a relative or friend. George Simpson is the only one of her brothers whose signature appears, so the family presumes that he was still in Maine at that time.

Mary Elizabeth Simpson Sperry, sixth from the right, photographed with the Women's Board of the 1915 Panama Pacific International Exposition.

Mary traveled by steamship or ferryboat from San Francisco to Stockton, and it was while visiting in that area that she met Austin Sperry. (After leaving Vermont for the gold fields of California, Austin had started the Sperry Flour Company in Stockton in 1852.)

The marriage of Austin and Mary took place in 1862, when the bride was twenty-nine. The Sperrys had two sons, both engineers, and two daughters, one a medical doctor and the other a musician.

Mary's own career as a suffragette developed in the late 1800s, and her name appears as treasurer on the letterhead of the California State Woman's Suffrage Educational Association.

A San Francisco newspaper article published around 1895 describes the approaching visit of leading suffragettes Susan B. Anthony and the Reverend Ann H. Shaw. They were to present lectures at the Sequoia Hotel and at the Alhambra Theater. Among the committee members listed is Mrs. Austin Sperry. In June 1916, when she was eighty-three, Mary was presented with a letter opener in appreciation of her presidency of the Susan B. Anthony Club.

A family story relates that during the San Francisco earthquake of 1906 the family boarded Andrew's lumber schooner at Pier 11 and went out on the bay, where they watched the city burn.

Along with this quilt, five others remain that are the work of Mary and/or her two daughters. The present owner is Mary's great-granddaughter.

Sampler of Flowers and Fruit

Not all California immigrants felt a loss at the breaking of family ties by moving west. Some deliberately severed their relationships, looking for a new start and a new life free of expectations and obligations. When C. C. West traveled from Baltimore, Maryland, to California by train in 1900, he came alone and hoped to leave his family behind forever. Among the few treasured possessions he brought with him was this Album Sampler quilt of fruits and flowers. He carefully preserved the quilt itself, but provided his descendants with no information about the quilter, her name, or her relationship to him.

According to family stories, C.C. ("Unc") abandoned his wife and children to come West to visit his friend, railway magnate "Lucky" Baldwin, whose girlfriend/mistress C.C. met and married. The Wests moved first to Porterville, where their only son, C. C. West, Jr., was born. They later moved to northern California, where C.C. invested in the aviation industry. The quilt passed from "Unc" to his son, "Westy," and on through three more generations.

A highly skilled quiltmaker fashioned this quilt's magnificent border in a reverse-appliqué Feather design. Her handwork throughout is exquisite, and she possessed a fine sense of design and color. Family recollections state that "Aunt Mary," C.C.'s great-granddaughter, lived on the East Coast and inherited an identical quilt from another branch of the family. When she moved west from Maine, the quilt was

49

Sampler of Flowers and Fruit with Feather Border, 1850–1870, made in Maryland. 97″ x 97″. Quiltmaker unknown. Detail included. Collection of The Rowley Family.

deemed too fragile to move with her, so she sold it to a collector who in turn sold it to a museum.

A recent issue of *Christie's* features a cover photograph of a quilt attributed to Mary Evans, who is credited as the maker of many of the superb appliqué motifs in the Baltimore Album quilts of the 1850s.[42] It has a border nearly identical to this quilt's, but the arrangement of album blocks differs. Both quilts are from Maryland, and the similarity of the remarkable borders piques our curiosity about the quiltmakers. Were they friends who shared patterns? Were they one and the same person? Were they related?

In spite of C.C.'s intention to cut family ties by starting a new life in California, the quilt has served as a tangible link in rejoining separated descendants. The present owner is a great-great-grandchild of the C.C. who brought this quilt to California.

Whig Rose/Tulip

In 1826, when Mary Powell moved from her Brethren family farm in Bracken County, Kentucky, to Clermont County in Ohio, the twenty-five-mile trip by team and wagon must have seemed a great distance from home. She was twenty-one and newly married to Calvin S. Beck, a farmer. The first of her eight children was born when she was twenty-three and the last when she was forty-nine. Two died as infants, one as a teenager, and three in their twenties. Only two survived her.

The change from one appliqué pattern to another, although abrupt, is carefully worked into the overall design of Mary's quilt. If the Carolina Lilies, in pots, are assumed to be at the bottom of the quilt, then the scallops on the right and left borders are not symmetrically matched. The four-flowered designs also vary, some bursting forth in a scalloped red arc, others with a smooth curve.

We know from her work that Mary was extremely skilled in her needlework. We can also see that while traditional, she was not conventional in her execution of arrangement. The brightness of the colors, the overall cheerful aspect of the quilt, and the hearts on the flowerpots might suggest a joyful life. However, in 1927, Mary's granddaughter found a concealed drawer beneath a shelf on one end of Mary's trunk. In that drawer was a letter written seventy-five years earlier, along with a tiny lace baby cap, an old parasol, and a leather Bible printed in the Old English style. The letter said, in part:

> *Dec. 3, 1848*
>
> *In my own handwrite poor as it may be, I Mary Beck will write a few lines concerning my married life. Twenty-two years and one month since I have been trying married life but I have had little comfort or happiness and very much sorrow and trouble have I been acquainted with in that time. Many tears have been shed....Many a time a see my nearest relative or best friends come, would have to wipe up my tears and put on as good a face as I could...I have thought many times that a steamboat could not run under such a burden as I have had to carry...no friend on earth could know my condition...Still I say "My grace is sufficient"...It is my great consolation that one day I shall leave these toilings and sorrows and go to my rest.*
>
> *Mary Beck (wife)*

Mary lived another thirty-three years after writing the letter.

Her quilt came to California in response to a dream that her granddaughter, Mary Lutisha Davis, had when she was forty-one. The dream was described by Wesley Davis, Mary Lutisha's husband:

> Mary, the children's dear mother, had the measles. She wanted to come to California but she was too weak to make the trip. As she grew weaker she

Top: Whig Rose Variation; *bottom:* Tulip Variation. 1850–1870, made in Ohio. 81″ x 82″. Quiltmaker: Mary Powell Beck (1805–1881). Detail included. Collection of Edward and Lorraine Davis.

went into a trance...she began making arrangements...told me to go upstairs and pack the trunks. She was "off to California"...eating fruit from the trees the land agent had told us about...She told us of the beautiful valley...and spoke of electric lights.[43]

She died shortly after, in 1911, after requesting that Wesley take their four children to California. In 1912, Wesley and the children arrived in Sutter County, having traveled by team and wagon, and by train. One of the children on that trip later inherited the quilt and passed it on to his son, the great-great-grandchild of the maker.

Buds and Leaves

When her parents died of the black plague in Ulm, Germany, in 1843, Rosina was nine years old. She left Ulm to live with an aunt and uncle who emigrated to America in 1844. They settled in Ohio, where Rosina stayed until her marriage to William Fredrick Widman in 1850, when she was sixteen.

William Fredrick Widman cut the fabric pieces for Rosina's quilt as they traveled to California via the Isthmus of Panama.

Soon after their marriage, the Widmans boarded a ship on the East Coast and sailed to the mouth of the Chagres River to cross the Isthmus of Panama. The ship anchored near the native village of Chagres (on the opposite bank an American town of the same name had sprung up in 1849 to offer hotels, saloons, and agents for the river travelers).

Once the steamers anchored at Chagres, passengers and their baggage were usually transported in native dugouts for a fifty-mile trip up the river. The trip took two to three days, with evening shelter sought in native houses along the river's bank. The river trip completed, the travelers transferred themselves and their belongings to mules that carried them on the final one-day journey to the western coast. There they connected with the ship that completed their passage to the California coast.[44]

It was on the Widmans' long trip to California that this appliqué quilt was begun and later finished in San Francisco. William cut the pieces and Rosina sewed as they traveled. "I know this because a woman who was a little girl on the same journey with Rosina and William told Rosina's granddaughter about the trip many years later when she finally saw the quilt completed."[45] Buttonhole stitches add spikey edges to the large leaves and wreaths while the buds are blind stitched. An overall hanging-diamond quilting pattern is augmented in outline quilting in the border.

The 1852 San Francisco directory listed Rosina as a dressmaker. The Widmans made their permanent home in San Francisco, where two sons and two daughters were born to them. The oldest son became an actor; the youngest owned a silver mine. A reflection, perhaps, of their mother's interest in sewing, the older daughter managed a millinery and dressmaking shop, and the younger worked in a dress store.

This quilt is presently with a great-granddaughter of Rosina's, who received it from an aunt whose wish it was to see it remain in the family.

Rosina Catherine Widman pieced her quilt en route to California from Ohio. She is pictured here with her son in a daguerreotype at San Francisco. c. 1855.

Sunburst

An Oroville, California, antiques shop displayed this quilt until it was purchased in 1976 as a gift for the present owner. A card sewn to the back of the quilt reads:

Made by Harriet E. Smith in the year of 1847 at New Madrid, Mo. Brought across plains in covered wagon in 1850 by the Ruddle family. Margaret R. Barfield was a sister to Mrs. Smith, all Merced Co. people.
      Signed by Flora N. Barfield, June 1937
      Merced, California

Buds and Leaves, 1850–1875, made en route to California. 80″ x 81″. Quiltmaker: Rosina Catherine Elizabeth Hummel Widman (1843–1875). Detail included. Collection of Mildred Breitbarth.

Sewing kit used by Rosina Widman when she traveled west via the Isthmus of Panama in 1849 or 1850.

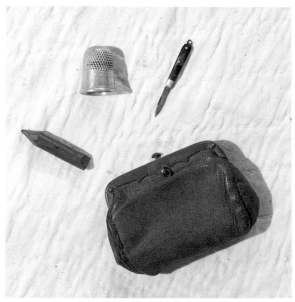

Sunburst with Evening Star sashing, family name: Sunflower, 1845–1880, made in Missouri (?). 88″ x 94″. Quiltmaker: Harriet E. Smith. Collection of Gayle Ryan.

If Harriet Smith was a sister of Margaret Barfield, then both were part of the family born to Margaret and John Ruddle in Missouri. The first member of the family to come west was a son of Margaret and John's, also named John Ruddle. At nineteen, he crossed the plains from Missouri, arrived in Los Angeles, and moved to the Merced area with the conviction that the future was more in farming than in gold. It was 1850, and while he may have brought the quilt with him, it is more likely that it was brought by the family at a later time.

John Ruddle (the son) acquired land in California, then traded it to his father for the farm in Missouri. He returned to Missouri and traded the farm for cattle, which he drove to California. Since his parents moved west, and two of his siblings are also known to have lived in the Merced area, family possessions may have come with them in the 1854 move.

One sister married and lived in the area, as did a brother who was believed to have been a victim of the desperado Joaquin Murietta and his gang.

While local records offer details about John Ruddle and his sister Margaret Barfield, no mention has been found of a Harriet E. Smith. Perhaps she was the oldest sibling, already married and settled in Missouri when the others emigrated. John Ruddle's obituary does not mention her at all, so either she did not survive him, she was not his sister, or they simply forgot her. Could she have sent the quilt along with the family members moving West as a remembrance of her? If so, why did Flora Barfield say they were "all Merced [County] people"?

Possibly the quilt was made in Missouri and brought here, as the quilt's note emphatically suggests. However, estimates of the quilt's age suggest it was made at a slightly later date, and therefore, in the Merced area. No known records point to Harriet Smith's having lived there.

Wherever Harriet was, her indigo-and-white quilt is in exceptionally fine condition, telling us that it has been carefully handled for all of its one hundred plus years. It appears to have been quilted by several different people, since stitches vary from very fine to less than fine.

The diagonally set sunburst blocks alternate with small Evening Stars at the intersections of the sashings. An extraordinary border, offset on one edge, sustains the precision of this pieced quilt.

Star of Bethlehem

When the Civil War took William Campbell away from his farm in Iowa, his wife started a quilt, pieced from hundreds of mid-nineteeth-century fabrics. Sadie Ellen Condron Campbell continued her sewing throughout the four-year duration of William's absence. The variety of quilting patterns (including diagonal lines, diamonds, and crosshatch) was matched by the diversity of her materials.

She worked with the help of her mother-in-law, Sarah Douglas Campbell (first cousin of Stephan A. Douglas), who did the quilting. William returned from the war, and a year later, in 1866, Sadie gave birth to their daughter, followed eleven years later by a son.

The quilt took a roundabout route to California. It was first given by Sadie to her daughter, Lillian Campbell Sparling, who had married and moved to Oklahoma. Lillian also made many quilts, and when she was later widowed, she supported herself and her son and daughter as a milliner. Lillian's daughter Hazel married Mr. Gosney, a homesteader, and with them this Star of Bethlehem traveled to Oregon. Lillian's son, Cecil, married and opened a Red and White grocery store in Oklahoma. He died on the day of his daughter Colleen's birth. His widow later married a miner, moved to Wyoming, and then to California; they settled, along with Colleen, in Chico.

Aunt Hazel Gosney, living in Oregon, accompanied her husband, now a plasterer, as he traveled up and down the West Coast. On one of these trips to California, she paid a visit to her niece, Colleen. She subsequently brought the quilt

Star of Bethlehem, family name:
Civil War Quilt, 1850–1875, made
in Iowa. 72″ x 72″. Quiltmakers:
Sarah Douglas Campbell (1812–
1905) and Sadie Ellen Condron
Campbell (1838–1886). Collection
of Coleen Vee Sparling Smith.

Prince's Feather Variation, family
name: Princess Feather, 1860,
made in Ohio. 86″ x 86″. Quiltmaker: Sarah Ann Drake Terry
(1838–1903). Collection of Shirley
A. Estrada.

by car in the 1930s to present to Colleen, who was the great-granddaughter of Sadie, the quilt's maker.

Prince's (Princess) Feather Variation

Before serving in the Civil War as a sergeant, George Terry married Sarah Ann Drake in Warren County, Ohio, in 1859. After his service, George returned to his work as a cabinetmaker and carpenter, and Sarah Ann gave birth to their only child, David.

Sarah Ann made this quilt around the time of her marriage; it was finished and dated in 1860. Little is known of her life, other than her birth date of 1838. Her choice of pattern and color, while popular for that period, is also an exuberant one. Between the feathers, the twenty-two-year-old quilter used eight different floral arrangements. Two have yellow birds perched among the leaves. Green and red birds nestle in the vines of a border design organized to make its way around the corners in a symmetrical pattern. Sarah fashioned a unique and personal interpretation of a well-known Feather pattern. Her appliqué is carefully whipstitched, and the background is quilted in an overall pattern of half-inch squares.

Sarah Ann's son inherited the quilt, and in the 1930s he moved to California, seeking a better climate for his health. He brought the quilt with him by car.

Whole-Cloth Stuffed Work

Born in Dublin, Ireland, in 1825, Isabella Armitage came with her parents to Nashville, Tennessee. From there her brother went west; in San Francisco he gave permission to Seth Louis Shaw to write to Isabella, whom Seth had met briefly in Tennessee. A long correspondence ensued, culminating in a proposal of marriage. Isabella accepted Seth's proposal, sailed around the Horn, and arrived in San Francisco in 1855, where she stayed at her brother's home to await Seth's arrival from farther north.

Seth had been attracted to California by the gold rush in 1849, but found it "not to his liking" and moved to San Francisco to pursue his vocation as a daguerreotype artist. With his brother, Stephen, a portrait painter, he later led a group of men north to a fertile area where the ferns grew eight feet tall. It was there that he founded Ferndale in 1852, became a farmer, and wrote his bride-to-be in Tennessee, "I am building a little cottage for you." The cottage was a beautifully appointed fourteen-room Victorian Gothic, fashioned after the House of Seven Gables described in Nathaniel Hawthorne's classic novel.

Seth's plan was to go to San Francisco, meet Isabella, and marry her. Unfortunately, the crop of potatoes upon which he was depending to finance the trip spoiled when the ship on which they were loaded failed to leave Port Kenyon, near Ferndale, as scheduled. The crop the following year proved successful, and Seth went at last by ship to San Francisco, where in 1857 he married Isabella and brought her back to Ferndale to their new home.

Potato growing must have proved successful, as freight listings twenty years later still included "661 sks [sacks] spuds" in November; two weeks later another 686 sacks; and 976 in December. By then, Seth's business had expanded into a remarkably diversified operation. He also shipped oats, barley, butter, tallow, sauerkraut, fresh fish, turkeys, dressed hogs, salmon, hides, pork, staves, coops of chickens, apples, and deer skin.

The Shaws lost their first two babies at birth, but in 1861 their only surviving son, Joseph Armitage, was born. It was for him that the white whole-cloth baby quilt was made. A large feather wreath, finely quilted and stuffed, forms a central design. Flowers and leaves, outlined and stuffed, are surrounded with diagonal lines and diamonds.

Isabella and Seth took in and reared two young American Indian girls, Swannee

Isabella Armitage Shaw about the time she made her all-white quilt. c. 1860.

Etching of the Ferndale home built by Seth Louis Shaw for his wife, Isabella, in 1854.

Whole-Cloth Stuffed Work, family name: The Shaw Cradle Quilt, 1860–1861, made in California. 35″ x 35″. Quiltmaker: Isabella Armitage Shaw (1825–1899). Collection of Betty Genzoli.

Mariner's Compass, Sunburst, 1867, made in California. 77″ x 87″. Quiltmakers: Susan A. Grant Hudson Grimes (1792–1871) and Martha Margaret Grimes Clark Strother (1836–?). Collection of Nel L. Estill.

Susan A. Grant Hudson Grimes, who pieced her intricate Mariner's Compass quilt in 1867.

Martha Grimes Clark Strother, daughter of Susan Grimes, who participated in the making of the Mariner's Compass when she was thirty-one, is on the right holding her purse and a pennant. On the left is Martha's daughter, Nellie Clark Lovelace, and other family members, probably Nellie's children.

and Biddy, who kept house for them. They were buried with the Shaws in the family mausoleum in Ferndale. In spite of the friendliness of most of the local Indians, Isabella had "secret areas" built into the back stairway where she hid her jewelry whenever any Indians approached the house.

The quilt is presently owned by the great-granddaughter of the maker.

Mariner's Compass

In December 1792, Susan A. Grant was born in Pennsylvania to Rachel Miller Kelly and Noah Grant, who was a tanner and farmer. Susan's brother was the father of Ulysses S. Grant, making her the future president's aunt.

Susan's marriage in 1815 to Baily Washington Hudson, a farmer and merchant, ended with his death just ten years later. She was living in Maysville, Kentucky, with her five young sons and a daughter, all of whom she raised to adulthood. The varied occupations of her sons included a mayor and minister to Guatemala, who was instrumental in Lincoln's nomination; a steamboatman, cattleman, and wharfmaster; a tanner; a lieutenant colonel with Grant's forces; and a soldier. Susan's one daughter is listed as a "benefactress."

In 1831, at age thirty-nine, Susan remarried, to Henry Grimes. They had two children, born in Ohio, the second, Martha, arriving when Susan was forty-four. They moved to West Virginia in 1849, then came west via wagon train and settled in Grand Island, California. The name of the town has since been changed to Grimes.

The quilt shows remarkable skill in both piecing and quilting, as well as a flexible approach regarding the corners of the square and diamond border. The Compass designs are enhanced with quilted concentric circles, and a running feather borders the two sides. Between the pieced blocks, open areas are filled with foliage and basket patterns. It is dated 1867, and was completed when Susan was seventy-five and her daughter Martha, who participated in its making, was thirty-one. Susan was again widowed two years later.

The quilt's present owner is the great-great-granddaughter and the great-granddaughter of the women who made it.

Rose Wreath

In 1905, the Granger family (including three young children) left Phillipsburg, Kansas, and came to California in a Pullman train. They also hired a boxcar, filled half of it with corn, and reserved the other half for family furniture and possessions. When the train pulled into Orange, California, the furnishings were safely unpacked, the corn was sold, and William David Granger established a new bank—The Orange Savings.

Among those possessions that the Grangers packed into the boxcar was a prized quilt that had been given to Ella Granger as a wedding present. It is believed that the maker of this exquisite work was Elvira Pearson (Aunt Ella), who was born in Pennsylvania in 1847 and married at twenty-five to a Mr. Mendenhall. The Mendenhalls had moved to Kansas, where Aunt Ella was a noted quiltmaker at the Friend's Settlement, then a Quaker community in Phillipsburg.

Described as a "tiny woman," Aunt Ella had no children of her own. It is believed that she gave the quilt to her niece and namesake, Ella Pearson Granger, on the occasion of the latter's marriage in 1872 to William, a Kansas senator and banker.

A family pamphlet, written in the 1930s by Ella Granger's brother, states the following about Aunt Ella:

> She is now in her 84th year, has excellent health but her greatest drawback being poor eyesight, which prevents her now from doing the beautiful needlework in which she spent so many happy hours.[46]

As a Quaker, Ella Granger eschewed fancy things; she did not even accept a

Rose Wreath, family name: The Box Car Quilt, 1860–1875, made in Kansas. 95″ x 96″. Quiltmaker: Elvira (Ella) Matilda Mendenhall (1847–1938). Detail included. Collection of Florence Tomblin.

Castor Bean Quilt, 1860–1880,
made in Virginia. 64″ x 80″. Quiltmaker: Lucy Linzy Pate Dukes
(1807–1890 ?). Collection of Jean T.
Danielson.

Basket of Lilies, 1860–1880, made
in Arkansas. 76″ x 67″. Quiltmaker:
Mary Jane Hopper (1852–1886).
Collection of Dorothy Atkins.

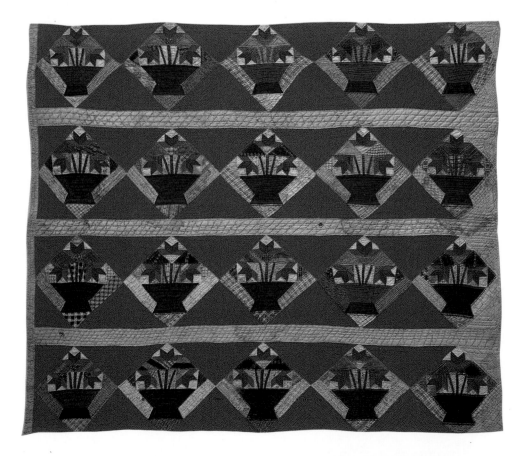

diamond ring when she married. Her aunt's quilt was the "fanciest thing she owned."

The extraordinary change from one border design to another is both disquieting and appealing in a piece brimming with precision. In blending her fine blind-stitch appliqué with elegant hand quilting, the quiltmaker produced a treasure that has passed in almost perfect condition through four generations. After quilting it with feather wreath and crosshatching, she finished its edge in piping. Aunt Ella was the great-great-grandaunt of the current owner.

Castor Bean

An 1822 marriage ceremony in Virginia united Lucinda Linzy Pate, age fifteen, with Andrew Dukes, a farmer. The couple remained in Virginia, where Lucinda had been born, and raised a family there.

Lucinda, Andrew, and the children later traveled west in a two-wheeled oxcart from Virginia to Fort Dearborne, then to Shelly County, Iowa. Lucinda died there between 1880 and 1890, and the quilt remained in Iowa until 1943, when it was sent by train to California. The current owner is the great-great-great-granddaughter of Lucinda, and the quilt has gone from mother to eldest daughter through the generations.

Information passed down in the family suggests that Lucinda made the white fabric, carding all the cotton herself, spinning the thread, and weaving it. The blue calico was purchased. The close parallel lines of a quilted shell pattern contrast to the bold lines of this sturdy hand-appliquéd Castro Bean, believed to be an original design of Lucinda's.

Basket of Lilies

This unusual Basket of Lilies was pieced in Arkansas by Mary Jane Hopper in the late nineteenth century. She was married and raised four or five children before her death, when her only daughter was eight years old. Some years later, when the daughter, Pruda, married, she carried this memento of her mother with her to Oak Grove, Arkansas; later to Apache, Arizona; and finally to California's San Joaquin Valley in 1914.

The striking indigo and orange of this bold quilt reveal a quiltmaker of resolute and vigorous spirit. Tangible evidence of the quilter's purpose is seen in the sturdy construction and firm quilting, which tell us that this quilt was meant to withstand use, as it has for over one hundred years. Its well-worn condition conveys that it was indeed valued for its durability and warmth, but perhaps it survived because it is all that remains to tell us about Mary Jane. The lilies are hand-pieced, and within the orange triangles, she quilted concentric squares. The quilting in the pieced blocks echoes the shapes of lilies and baskets.

A letter from her father, with the letterhead "M. T. Hopper, Farmer and Fruit Grower, Alpena Pass, Arkansas," sent to Mary in 1913, includes recipes for croup and "baithing the feet."

Having passed from mother to only-daughter for four generations, the quilt now belongs to the maker's great-granddaughter. She has several other quilts of Mary Jane's as well, including the fragile remnants of her wedding quilt.

Whig Rose

An obliterating cloud of anonymity lurks near every quiltmaker whose name is not included on, or in, her work. Families shift, separate, and migrate; notes, pinned to quilt backs, get lost; relatives can no longer recall details; interest in quilts dwindles as life-changing events take on a greater momentary importance. This unsigned quilt, like many others, exposes puzzles and gives clues, but offers few answers.

Whig Rose Alternated with Blocks
of Stars and Hearts, 1855–1885,
made in California. 77″ x 87″.
Quiltmakers: Catherine Amanda
Peterman Thomas Plymire (1819–
1891) and/or Mary Jane Sligar
(1847–1877). Collection of Audrey
W. Johnson.

In 1858, the widowed Catherine Amanda Peterman Thomas of Ohio married her second husband, Samuel Plymire. Samuel had left Pennsylvania at age thirty to join the '49ers, and after spending time near Oroville, on the Feather River, he went prospecting in Australia. Returning to the East, he married Catherine and brought his bride on the long trek to California. From Ohio, Catherine's mother, Elizabeth Peterman, wrote: "It seems a long time since I saw you and I fear I shall never see you again if you do not come home soon. It is now six years since you bade us all an affectionate farewell to go to that far off land California."[47]

Catherine's son from her first marriage, George Washington Thomas, wed Mary Jane Sligar at the St. Nicholas Hotel in Oroville in 1865. Born in Kentucky, Mary Jane had come to Missouri with her parents and seven siblings when she was about nine, and moved on to California about four years later. She was eighteen when she married, and in the early 1870s she was away from home due to an illness. In a letter to one of her several children, she comments, "I hope you are going to school and learning fast; [your] Ma is getting better and the doctor says Ma will get well and then we will all be happy again."[48]

Her letters refer to the presence of the children's grandmother, possibly Catherine, with them at home. Mary Jane died at twenty-nine. It was to her daughter Katherine that this treasured quilt was passed.

The abundance of hearts suggests that this quilt may have been made as a wedding quilt. One family recollection is that the quilt came to California around the Horn. Another is that the quilt was made by either Mary Jane or Catherine. Reconciling these with the estimate of the quilt's age reveals discrepancies.

Because Mary Jane left Kentucky at age nine and came to California overland from Missouri at thirteen, she could not have brought it around the Horn. Neither is it likely, considering her age, that she made it before coming to California.

If Catherine made the quilt, and even our earliest estimate of the quilt's age is accurate, then it could not have been made before her trip west. Had it been made earlier, it might have come by ship, though it is believed that Samuel Plymire had crossed overland on his earlier trip. Catherine would not have made it as a wedding quilt before her departure, since Mary Jane was only eleven or twelve when Catherine moved to California.

Elizabeth Peterman, in her letter to Catherine, refers to the possible release of William (assumed to be her son), of the Army of the Potomac, from his rebel captors. She also refers to the six-year lapse since Catherine's departure. These references indicate 1864, or possibly 1865, as the date of the letter, putting Catherine in California the year of her marriage or the next (1858 or 1859). Unless the estimate of the quilt's age is in error, it is unlikely that the quilt was made in Ohio or that it arrived via the Horn. The quilt was, therefore, probably made near Gridley, California, by either of the two women.

Blocks of five stars set alternately with Whig Rose blocks have appliquéd hearts at their centers. Quilted hearts border the blocks and fill the areas between stars, and each of the central gold stars is surrounded by a quilted wreath.

This handsome, spirited quilt now belongs to the great-granddaughter of Mary Jane Sligar.

Oak Leaf and Reel

Clarissa Jane Edsall's life began near Mansfield, Ohio, in 1826. In 1841, at age fifteen, she married the Reverend Lorenzo Waugh, eighteen years her senior, a traveling elder of the Methodist church in Missouri.

The privations of their itinerant life were many, and by 1851, when Clarissa was twenty-six, both she and Lorenzo were in broken health. With their three sons, they crossed the plains with an ox train to California, settling four miles from what is now Petaluma, on a quarter section of land given to them by General Vallejo.

As there was no church in this new community, their home was opened for

Oak Leaf and Reel, Friendship Quilt, 1872, made in California. 72" x 79½". Quiltmaker: Clarissa Jane Edsall Waugh (1827–1887). Collection of Hannah R. Zoulas.

Prince's (Princess) Feather with Stars, 1865–1880, made in Ohio. 89" x 89". Quiltmaker: Elizabeth ("Betsy") Buckles Baugh (1828–1917). Collection of Atlanta Baugh Bussey.

preaching and social religious meetings. A daughter was born there, and a fourth son, who died at age nine. It was during this period that Clarissa made her quilt top. Embroidered on it is the inscription, "Made by C. J. Waugh A. D. 1872," and four signatures appear on each block. The Oak Leaf and Reel, a graphic composition of brown prints with blue and varied borders in prints and stripes, was finished years later by W. F. and F. C. Sayles in Pawtucket, Rhode Island. Both blind stitch and whipstitch were used in the appliqué.

Lorenzo's autobiography (1883) is an "engrossing conglomeration of growing up in West Virginia, study for the ministry, Indian and buffalo excitement on the way westward, constant sermons about the evils of liquor and tobacco, acrostic poetry, life in California and memories of people met along the way."[49] It also includes a bitter discussion of the "settler leagues" and their opposition to Spanish land grants. The "settler leagues" were instrumental in the drive to gain possession of land-grant territories for California's rapidly growing population. Lorenzo had been dispossessed of the property, given to him by Vallejo, that he and Clarissa had held and worked for nine years, which prompted his bitterness toward the leagues. Vallejo's original offer was made good when he provided the Edsalls with land from his own holdings to replace those lost.

Clarissa's eldest son, John, carried mail for the pony express between Sacramento and Petaluma, and a son-in-law captained the *San Joaquin No. 4*, a large towboat on the Sacramento River.

Clarissa's obituary, which appeared in a San Francisco newspaper in 1887, states:

Clarissa Jane Waugh, quiltmaker, and her husband, Reverend Lorenzo Waugh. c. 1860.

> Even their house was a model of neatness and quiet, as well as of a generous and unostentatious hospitality. Though never demonstrative, Sister Waugh was ever ready and prepared for every needed work....She was truly triumphant in her death. She embraced her children and gave them a message of dying love...it is pleasant to know that what Mr. Wesley said of the Methodists of his time is true of these—"they die well."

The quilt has remained in the family, passing from one generation to the next. It is currently owned by Clarissa's great-great-granddaughter.

Prince's (Princess) Feather with Stars

Elizabeth (Betsy) Buckles learned sewing as a child, and family history recounts that she was first given carpet rags to stitch on. Piecing quilts, along with doll clothes, came next, and when sufficient skills were learned, she began quilting (removing unacceptable stitches!).

Elizabeth made this Prince's (Princess) Feather with Stars before her marriage in anticipation of her future home. Since she didn't marry until she was forty-one, there was ample time for her to develop the exquisite skills used in both the complex appliqué and the quilting pattern of this piece. Her border treatment and the fineness with which she maneuvered corners are exceptional. Betsy owned one of the early Wheeler and Wilson sewing machines, but used it only in sewing dresses and making trousers. Her quilts were made by hand.

In 1869, Betsy married a widower, Jacob Baugh, who was a blacksmith and farmer, and the father of three sons. Betsy raised the children and spent her entire life in Champaign County, Ohio.

After Betsy's death, a son and his family came to California on a visit. His daughter, Atlanta, stayed to attend UCLA, and in 1935, on the occasion of her marriage, she received her grandmother's quilt.

The Grant Quilt/Flying Birds/Birds in the Air

The family Bible, in which Adam Lohry recorded family history, listed his marriage to Susan Deering in 1843. Born in Kentucky nineteen years earlier, Susan

Flying Birds, Birds-in-the-Air, family name: The Grant Quilt, 1868–1878, made in California. 62½″ x 81″. Quiltmaker: Susan Deering Lohry (1824–1884). Collection of Norma C. Smith. *Note:* Back of quilt, folded to show front.

Blazing Star, 1870–1875, made in California. 79″ x 80″. Quiltmaker: Elizabeth Garrigus Chandler (1853–1877). Collection of Thelma A. Keyes.

Chimney Sweep, Album Block, family name: The John Brown Quilt, 1870–1880, made in California. 93″ x 81″. Quiltmaker: Adah Bingham McKelvey (1830?–1890?). Collection of Webb McKelvey.

and Adam left that state for Missouri three years after their marriage. In 1853, they set out for the West in a covered wagon with their baby and four small children, all under eight years.

The peak of the gold rush was in 1852, and by 1853 over one hundred thousand prospectors had swarmed into the new state. They represented every state in America and every country of Europe. In one year they retrieved eighty-one million dollars worth of gold from the slopes of the Sierra.

When the Lohrys arrived in Unionville (later called Lotus), California, they opened a general store, and just a few years later built a more permanent structure in brick. Their brick home, built a year later in 1858, was burned to the ground when a four-year-old child, carrying a candle, accidentally set the curtains on fire. The house was rebuilt that same season.

Five more children were born in Unionville. Adam's handwritten notes in the Bible include two infant deaths and mention of an older daughter's elopement (her name is outlined in black).

In 1880, Adam committed suicide by drowning himself in the American River, which ran through the back of their property. He was distraught over the theft of gold left in the safe at his store for safekeeping by local miners. His son-in-law was convicted and sent to state prison for the crime.

In 1880, Susan placed an ad in the Placerville *Mountain Democrat*, offering a fifty-dollar reward for the recovery of Adam's body. The ad ran for one month, but no follow-up article indicates any recovery. A family burial plot in the Lotus cemetery, however, contains a tall marker with Adam's name engraved on it. Beside this is the grave of a son who had died a few years earlier at age nineteen. Susan died several years after Adam, but no marker indicates her grave.

It was during her life in the brick house in Unionville that Susan made her Grant quilt, the back of which is of special interest. Salvaging remnants and scraps provided an important source of materials for quilts, and here is exceptional evidence of a salvage effort.

When Ulysses S. Grant ran for the U.S. presidency in 1868, supporters organized torchlight parades, which had been popular outdoor political events since the late 1830s. Flaming torches provided illumination for the marching supporters and, along with banners, created dramatic effects for the campaigns. Once its political role was concluded, this hand-painted banner was given new life as the backing for Susan's quilt. On the front of the quilt, scraps from family clothing yielded an array of browns for the pieced Flying Birds. It is machine-quilted in an Ocean Waves pattern with diagonal lines in the border.

Susan made this quilt when she was forty-four with the help of three of her daughters—Caroline, the eldest; Lucy, who married the son of the founder of Yountville; and Ann, who later worked on a Pacific Grove newspaper.

Perhaps Susan's quilt, which effectively combined political activities with domestic realities, influenced her five daughters. Besides Ann, two other daughters were involved with newspaper work—one who was a correspondent for a Williams, California, paper and one who worked for the *Sacramento Bee*.

The present owner of the quilt is Susan's great-granddaughter, who commented, "I admire [her] greatly. She crossed the plains with five small children and in California she had five more. I wonder how she could have done it."

Blazing Star

Angel's Camp was a rowdy, bustling center for immigrant miners when Elizabeth Garrigus was born there in 1853. Her parents had joined the gold rush and traveled to California by covered wagon. In Angel's Camp they were involved in mining as well as a grocery business. Elizabeth later attended Sacred Heart School in San Jose and then, to prepare herself for teaching, was one of the first students at San Jose Normal School in 1869 or 1870.

Elizabeth Garrigus, photographed about the time of her marriage. Santa Clara, California. 1873.

Elizabeth taught school in Pescadero, California, and it was probably there that she produced this Eight-Pointed Star quilt for her trousseau. After her marriage in 1871 or 1872 to Lafayette Chandler, she took the wedding quilt to her new home, where she later gave birth to a daughter. The child was only one and a half years old when her mother died of blood poisoning in 1877, at age twenty-four. The current owner of the quilt is a fourth cousin of the quiltmaker's husband.

The splendid, radiant stars of this quilt, now faded and worn, were hand-pieced, then hand-quilted with a crosshatch pattern. A fine line of piping separates the double border from the binding.

Chimney Sweep

Adah Bingham came to California from Pennsylvania around 1850 with her parents, sailing through the Caribbean to the Isthmus of Panama. As the trans-Panama railway was only begun in 1850, they would have taken small boats up the Chagres River and would then have transferred to mules for the remaining eighteen to twenty miles. This must have been an exotic trip through "the jungle, whose outward beauty made John Muir weep with delight when he first saw it."[50] The jungle's density, however, slowed the railway work, and "even on the sunniest day, men with torches had to precede those who hacked away the crowding, tangled plant growth, which teemed with bugs of all sizes and degrees of viciousness."[51]

After arriving in California and moving into the Central Valley, Adah's father started his ranch near Visalia. There Adah met the Reverend John McKelvey, who had come to California in 1849 or 1850. When he first arrived in California, McKelvey spent nearly five years in the gold fields before he decided to go into the ministry, for he had been converted to Christianity in Pennsylvania. He raised the necessary seventy-five dollars to join the Methodist Conference in San Francisco. His first assignment was in Mariposa, and his next in Visalia, where he met Adah and the Bingham family.

When Adah and John were married, their first home was a cabin that John built at the back of the Binghams' house, using available lumber from dry-goods shipping boxes. Their oldest son was born there in 1864, followed by another son and a "sister or two." Some time later, the family took a trip to Kern County in a mule-drawn stage. At one point in the journey, the mules jerked so violently that Adah's eighteen-month-old daughter fell from the stage and was run over.

Reverend McKelvey was a circuit-riding preacher, going out on horseback and staying in people's homes. In 1867, he was sent to Eureka, accompanied by Adah and the children. In time, he ministered to residents from French Camp to San Francisco, and built churches in many areas throughout the state.

It was when the McKelveys were in the Roanerville area that Adah, who planned the family's social events, held a quilting bee for the widow of John Brown. Mary Ann Brown, the abolitionist's second wife, had fled her New York home with four of his twenty children after John Brown was hanged as a traitor for his raid on the federal arsenal at Harper's Ferry, Virginia. The widow and her children had come by wagon train to Red Bluff, a journey that took an entire year. They arrived "a hungry, almost barefoot, ragged lot."[52] Mary Ann worked as a midwife, and two of her daughters taught black children in Proberta. (By 1875 there were seven thousand blacks in California. During the years after the Civil War, laws prohibiting their attendance at public schools were repealed through legislation, but in actual practice their total acceptance was frequently resisted.)

For her quilting party, Adah invited women supportive of the widow and sympathetic to her plight. Mary Ann and her daughters were the guests of honor; in attendance also were the thirty women who signed the quilt.

The women signed their names in the centers of the blocks. Whereas one block appears to be blank, in two the quilters have doubled up. Counting from the upper left, Mrs. John Brown signed block number 25, Miss Ellen Brown number 24, and

Miss Sadie Brown number 17. An inked metal stamp bearing the image of a spread-winged eagle above a cluster of arrows has provided an elaborate oval in which the quilters have entered their names.

Reverend McKelvey later became Bishop of Kern, Los Angeles, and Santa Barbara counties. When his health failed around 1888, he and Adah lived with their oldest son in the Los Angeles area, where Adah died two years later.

The quilt has remained in the family and is now owned by a great-grandson of the quiltmaker.

Double T

The health crusade of the 1840s (which advocated fresh air, exercise, comfortable clothing, and moderate diet), together with the movement for women's rights, provided the chief impetus in getting women into medical training. Family history relates that Mary Elizabeth Custis (Custiss) was a licensed physician studying in New York at the outbreak of the Civil War. By the 1850s there were several schools that admitted women—not, however, without obstacles and difficulties. Even after medical training, women found that few hospitals would admit them to their staffs. However, a medical degree was, in many states, license to practice.[53]

Women *were* accepted as nurses to aid the Union Army during the war, but only with much reluctance. They had to be "over thirty years of age, plain in appearance and dress, and . . . willing to subscribe to a host of regulations dictating almost every waking moment of their lives."[54] Still, northern women eagerly volunteered for hospital duty, while southern tradition did not encourage women to enter a "man's world."[55]

Mary Elizabeth Custis Compton Park with her horse, Harry, after her move to California. c. 1910.

Mary was born in 1842 on the family farm in Arlington, Virginia. Her maiden name, Custis, was a name clearly aligned with the South.[56] While attending school in the North, Mary chose to change her last name to Compton. Nevertheless, her home and family ties were in the South, her sympathies with the southern cause. It was a situation that led her to run medical supplies and drugs to the Confederate Army, for which the Union Army placed a bounty on her head.

Mary's engagement to an officer of the Confederate Army was cut short when he was killed in action before their marriage could take place. She was pregnant at the time, and whether or not her chosen name of Compton was also his name is not known. Her daughter, Laura, was born in 1865.

Mary later married a Mr. Park and assumed his name. She had no other children, and her daughter retained the Compton name until her own marriage. When family members came west to do construction work on railway stations in Oakland, Santa Cruz, and Fresno after the devastation of the 1906 earthquake, Mary also moved to California. As a widow, she lived with her daughter and son-in-law in Berkeley and Fresno, and died in 1925.

This Centennial quilt celebrates the Philadelphia Centennial Exposition of 1876 and includes a wonderful collection of rust-brown prints from that era, along with an American roller-print of the Liberty Bell in the sashing. The quilting utilizes both outline and diagonal patterns. Mary was apparently a prolific quiltmaker, and many of her works are in the possession of a great-great-grandson in New Jersey.

This quilt went to Mary's daughter, Laura, then to her granddaughter, and finally to her great-grandson, the current owner.

Star of Bethlehem

When Emma Shafer died in the 1919 flu epidemic, she left many quilts, among them this colorful star now owned by her granddaughter. What became of numerous others is unknown.

Emma Elizabeth Iteller was born in 1855 to Dutch parents in Northampton, Pennsylvania. At twenty-nine, she married widower Frederick Shafer, who owned

71

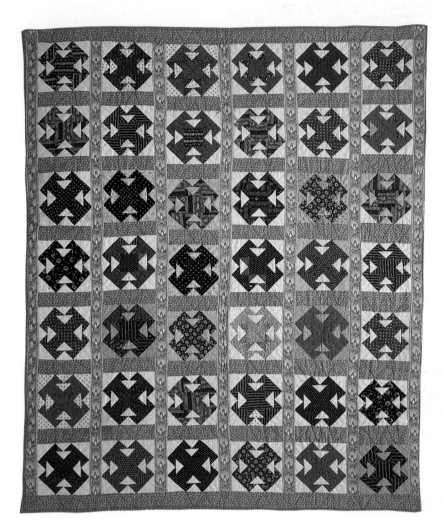

Double T, Maltese Cross, 1870–
1880, made in New Jersey. 77″ x
92½″. Quiltmaker: Mary Elizabeth
Custis (Custiss) Compton Park
(1842–1925). Detail included. Collection of Lawrence Rawson.

Star of Bethlehem with Peonies and Stars, 1870–1880, made in Pennsylvania. 80″ x 80″. Quilt-maker: Emma Elizabeth Heller Shafer (1855–1920s?). Collection of Esther L. Henley.

Tumbling Blocks, Baby Blocks, family name: Optical Illusion, 1870–1890, made in California. 67″ x 74″. Quiltmaker: Flora Lillie Leaman McIntyre (1856–1920). Collection of Evelyn P. Joslyn.

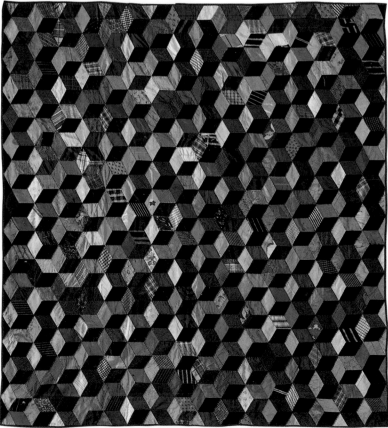

a flour mill and later became a farmer. It was after the death of Frederick's first wife that Emma had come to be his housekeeper and to care for his five children. After their marriage, Emma had four more children.

She made this quilt at Powerhouse Crossing, near Easton, in Pennsylvania Dutch country. Emma's frame was set up in the second-floor back room of her home, where she used the quilting skills taught her by her older sister. The diminutive Emma, who never weighed more than one hundred pounds, was an excellent cook and entertained often, especially at Sunday dinners. Her oldest son was put through seminary on Emma's "egg money."

This quilt was given by Emma to her daughter, and was then inherited by her granddaughter, who brought it to California in 1943 or 1944. The owner says, "It is the only tangible from a grandmother I never knew. It is family... into the past and the future."

Tumbling Blocks

Flora Lillie Leaman McIntyre, whose Optical Blocks quilt was raffled to benefit an ill miner.

After running fishing boats in Maine, Henry S. and Elvira Kimball Leamon sailed out of Bangor in May of 1854, around Cape Horn, and into San Francisco. Their first child was born just one month after their arrival. Perhaps two years later, they headed for Forbestown, where their daughter Flora Lillie was born. According to family history the Leamons had no shelter, having just arrived in this mining town, so Flora was born under a pine tree, delivered by an Indian woman. Flora grew up in Oroville, where her father prospected for gold and later became a ferryboat operator.

Flora's quilt is mentioned by her daughter in *One Woman's California*:

> In the pioneer camps at Morris Ravine the miners always looked after each other. About 1872–1873 one man became ill. The miners had a big meeting in front of Joe Hendley's cabin to take up a collection for him. My Mother donated a beautiful quilt to be raffled at this meeting which she made from a collection of silk ties. The old miner who won it gave it back to her.[57]

This optical Blocks top was pieced by Flora before her marriage, using silks she had gathered over several years. With leftovers from her tied quilt, Flora also made a pillow. Years later, when a child poked an exploratory finger through the pillow's fragile silk, it was discovered that the papers used in the English piecing of the block came from love letters written to Flora by Angus A. McIntyre, whom she had married in 1874. Angus had left farming on the East Coast to become a gold miner and mine owner. When Flora's seventh and youngest child was born in 1889, they were living in "the old Leamon Home" on Cherokee Road several miles out of Oroville.

Flora was widowed at thirty-three when Angus drowned in the West Branch of the Feather River during a heavy rainstorm. It was assumed that he lost his footing on a slick footbridge. Flora had lost two of her infant children, and when the youngest of the remaining five was five years old, she went to San Francisco, where she opened a boardinghouse in 1894 or 1895, about four years after Angus's death.

She had a little income from Angus's share in a mining partnership. Then when a longtime family friend bequeathed her a small house in Oroville, she sold it and used the proceeds to lease the third floor of a house on Van Ness Avenue in San Francisco. Besides space for her family, she had four beds in one room, and two double rooms, for renters. The married couples and single women to whom she rented—no single men allowed—could also board with her.

Flora cooked, and all the children helped with the cleaning and were assigned regular jobs. Only the oldest daughter, Mary, was exempt because she worked outside the home. Flora did her own washing, which she hung from the third-floor back porch. She ran the boardinghouse until 1906, when it was destroyed by the devasting fire that swept the city after the earthquake. One of her older daughters had married a doctor in Los Angeles, and he persuaded Flora to come there to live in a bungalow provided for her. She was taken care of by her children for the remainder of her life.

The quilt belongs to Flora's youngest daughter, now ninety-nine years old. She says: "[The quilt] hangs on my dining room wall, the silk in perfect condition and the colors bright." She will leave the quilt to the Butte County Pioneer Museum in Oroville.

Hole-in-the-Barn-Door

Fannie P. Towne was born in Norway, Maine, in 1816, where she was married, spent her entire life, and died. Her husband was Perry Dimon Judkins, a blacksmith whom she married in January 1837. Late that same year, the first of her four sons was born. The youngest appeared in the 1850 census (he was a year old) and does not reappear in 1860. Only two of the others survived her.

When Flora Judkins Cummings, daughter of Fannie's son Oliver Wendell Holmes Judkins, passed the quilt on to her daughter Edna, she attached this letter:

> *Dear Daughter*   *Dec. 1933*
> *A quilt your grandfather's mother made. I have had it 40 years. Have kept it as an heirloom. It never has been used but very little. May you enjoy it more than a new quilted quilt, like those being made these days. It may not be as handsome, but age gives it distinction. May this be a very merry Christmas to you and yours.*
> *Lovingly Mother,*
> *Flora Judkins Cummings*

Edna had married a Californian and returned home with him on their honeymoon trip in 1917. The quilt arrived by mail sixteen years later, when Flora sent it to her as a Christmas present.

Edna stored the quilt in a cedar chest made for her own daughter, who was given the chest and quilt upon her marriage. The quiltmaker was the great-great-grandmother of the present owner.

The wonderful variations of prints, plaids, and stripes in the Flying Geese border echo all the grays and roses of this engaging quilt. Hand-quilting outlines the pieced designs.

Tumblers

In 1893, Emogene Florence Woolsey Hart left Stafford, Kansas, and came by train to California with her husband and family, seeking better living conditions and a better climate. Emogene was twenty-two and had been married for three years to Frank Hart, a rancher and dairyman. Of English, German, and Choctaw heritage, she raised seven children to adulthood. Emogene is recalled by her family as being very religious and active in the Women's Temperance League.

According to family history, Emogene started the quilt when she was six years old, in 1877, in Brosley, Cass County, Missouri—a town that no longer exists. She learned quilting from her mother and grandmother. This Charm quilt contains 510 fabric patterns, with no two alike, and was worked on over a number of years. It left Missouri with fifteen-year-old Emogene when her family moved to Kansas, and was later brought to California when she and her husband moved west shortly after their marriage.

Emogene made other quilts as well, some of which are owned by her son, who received them in 1948. This machine-pieced top was finished and hand-quilted by an unknown quiltmaker in Santa Cruz in the 1940s. Emogene was widowed after

Emogene Florence Woolsey Hart at the time of her marriage to Frank Hart in 1890.

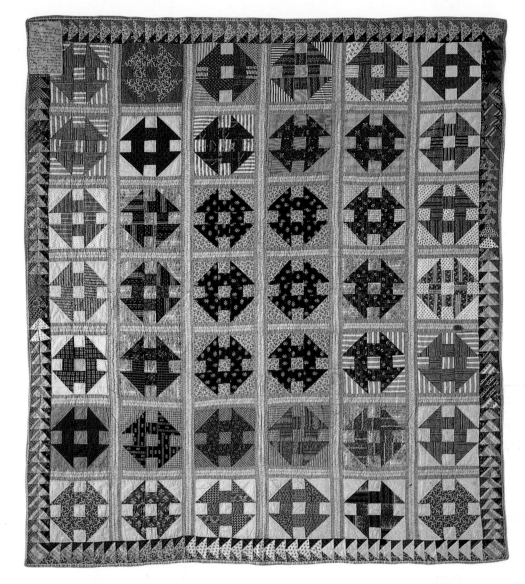

Hole-in-the-Barn-Door, Churn Dash, 1870–1890, made in Maine. 77″ x 88″. Quiltmaker: Fannie P. Towne Judkins (1816–1903). Collection of Mrs. Flora Borges.

Tumbler, Charm Quilt, 1876–1890, made in Missouri. 64″ x 80″. Quiltmaker: Emogene Florence Woolsey Hart Guymon (1871–1956). Collection of Donald C. Hart.

Evening Star, 1870–1890, made in Pennsylvania. 64″ x 77″. Quiltmaker unknown. Collection of Gail Taylor Moore.

fifty-two years of marriage, and then remarried when she was seventy-nine, to Samuel J. Guymon.

Evening Star

Quiltmakers' names are often lost as quilts travel hand to hand, state to state, and generation to generation. The only tangible evidence of a woman's life (other than her children) often exists only in her quilts.

This Star quilt, made in the late 1800s, offers that tangible evidence, but little information. The green fabrics are hand-dyed, the pieced blocks are well constructed, and it is undated and unsigned. The star blocks are hand-quilted in a grid pattern of squares with double diagonal lines over the plain blocks and the borders.

The quilt was purchased in 1970 from a cousin of General John Pershing. The cousin recalled that the quilt had come from the Pennsylvania family home of the Pershings, was then taken to Texas, and in about 1930 came to California. When the cousin decided to move back to Texas, the quilt was offered for sale.

Its present owner says, "I was particularly happy to be able to get this quilt because my youngest brother was born in 1918 and was named John Pershing Taylor."

Log Cabin

French-Canadians Bernard and Mary Lisset Berdau (Thiberdau) emigrated to Troy, New York, in 1835. Here were born Mary and Margaret, the seventh and eighth of the nine children in the family. When the girls were teenagers, the family moved to Livingstone County, Illinois. On her twentieth birthday, in 1862, Mary wed John Bearcroft in a double ceremony with her sister Margaret, who married Gilbert Wyman, an attorney and author.

Mary had one son, who died at sixteen. Margaret's three children were born in the 1860s and 1870s in Illinois.

This Log Cabin quilt in the Barn Raising design is believed to have been made by one of the sisters, or both; it went eventually to Margaret Berdau Wyman.

After twenty-five years of marriage, having moved previously to Marion County and later to Chicago, Margaret's family moved west, hoping to improve the health of Edna, the youngest daughter, then ten.

It was 1887 when the Wymans arrived in Oakland and moved into a house on 28th Avenue and 16th Street. Edna thrived and was later married in the family home. The quilt was passed down through Edna's family and is presently owned by a great-great-grandson of the quiltmaker.

Margaret Elizabeth Berdeau Wyman, whose move to California was prompted by her daughter's ill health. Photographed in Illinois. c. 1865.

Virginia Star

Cary Ann Miller left her native Virginia and married Elisha Massey Thomas in Little Rock, Arkansas, in 1854 or 1855. Just a year later, they joined Elisha's friend Captain Mat Sewell (who had accompanied an earlier immigrant train to California) on his next trip west. They traveled in an ox-drawn wagon with no springs, and endured many hardships. Although they were several times surrounded by Indians, the chiefs were always friendly with Sewell, and the party arrived at the California border without incident. As they neared the border, according to family recollections and records, Captain Sewell said, "I will hurry the train up a little so you will have a native son or daughter." And hurry they did. They crossed the border at sundown and their baby arrived at sunup, near Humboldt Sump in Calaveras County, just over the border. These recollections were recorded in 1888 by that daughter, Mary A. Thomas True, and were, she said, "as near as my parents recollect."

Wedding photo of Mary Ann Thomas and J. R. True. Yuba City, California. 1876.

Log Cabin, Barn Raising, 1870–1890, made in Illinois. 67″ x 69½″. Quiltmakers: Mary Berdeau Bearcroft (1842–?) and Margaret Berdeau Wyman (1843–1909). Collection of Dale Cary Nordling.

Virginia Star, 1870–1900, made in California. 73″ x 75″. Quiltmaker: Mary Ann Thomas True (1856–1945). Collection of Otto V. and Joyce T. Lund.

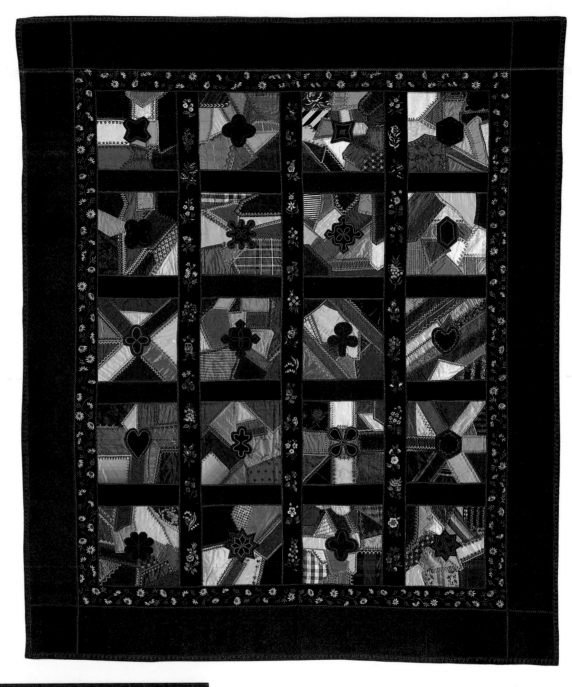

Sashed Crazy Quilt, 1880–1885, made in California. 72″ x 86″. Quiltmaker: Annie D. Fee Billups (1865–1943). Dolls illustrated at left were made by the quiltmaker. Collection of Millie Golden Webb.

Carbon paper with traced patterns, 8" wide by 30" long, found among the sewing tools of Mary Ann Thomas True.

Apparently, by the time of her birth, baby Mary was so used to the shaking and rocking of the wagon train that she was inconsolable without it! Thereafter, when the wagon stopped for meals, the parents alternated—one ate while the other "shook" the baby.

The Thomases settled near Angel's Camp, where Elisha mined. A second daughter was born there, and when she died at eight months, Cary "felt her taking so keenly" that they moved to Marysville, where Cary's older sister lived. Here a third girl was born, and a disastrous flood drowned much of their stock. Discouraged, they next moved to Sutter County, near General Sutter's Hock Farm. From there, they went farther west and bought a farm two miles from Yuba City.

Cary taught her daughters to sew, and some of Mary Ann's earliest work, made at age eight, is still in the family. Mary Ann was married in the family home in 1876 to James Rallings (or Rawlings) True, who had a ranch at Live Oak. In 1879 they arrived in Santa Cruz, and James worked as a teamster from Santa Barbara to the gold country. A year later, he finished their "cottage" on Ocean Avenue, and descendants of the Trues have lived there ever since.

In 1893, at age thirty-two, Mary Ann started a diary that she kept faithfully until the 1930s. Excerpts from her diary read:

> Mon. Jan. 2, 1893…Went to ride and to races. Washed. 2 quilts, one blanket and spread.
> Wed. Ap. 25 Rosa went downtown got me 31 yard satune for waist for $1.00 [Rosa lived with the family, helped with chores and children.]
> Thur. July 27. Rosa at home. Went with Mrs. Wilson up to Mrs. Wilkins to the Ladies Sewing Band.

Her Crazy work seemed to occupy her for some time, as evidenced by these fragmented diary entries:

> …got some crazy work patterns…went over to Mrs. M for her quilt for a pattern…Bertha came in to work on crazy work…wrote a letter home and worked on crazy block…finished the crazy patch block and pressed it—ready to send home…

The present owner says the quilt was not so much inherited as it was "just found" in the old family home. It was folded in a closet, and the family has surmised that it was one of the many surviving quilts made by Mary Ann. The quilt now belongs to the family of Cary Thomas's great-grandson.

Sashed Crazy Quilt

This well-ordered Crazy quilt was stitched by Annie D. Feė for her marriage in 1883. Born in Virginia City, Nevada, eighteen years earlier, she was two when her parents came by wagon train to Fort Bidwell. The fort was named for Major John Bidwell of the California Volunteers, who had led one of the first overland parties of settlers into California (the Bidwell-Bartleson train) in 1841. He discovered gold at Bidwell's Bar, used his money to buy land, and became a friend of General Sutter. The fort was established to hold in check any marauding Indians in northeastern California, southern Oregon, or western Nevada, and to protect the travel routes in that area. When the government established an Indian school and hospital there in the 1890s, it served as headquarters for the Fort Bidwell Indian Reservation.

Annie grew up in a log cabin on a cattle ranch run by her parents, then attended high school and, later, a finishing school in Berkeley. Her mother taught her to quilt when she was ten, and Annie apparently learned well, as this piece was finished before she was eighteen. Her marriage to Lafayette (Lafe) Billups that same year took her to another cattle ranch in the area, where she spent many more years in a log cabin. She gave birth to a son and a daughter.

80

The sashing of her quilt is embroidered in colorful details of sparkling contrast, and each block has an unusual central design. The luxurious fabrics and handwork must have graced the log cabin with a distinctive and elegant touch. Annie also created dolls that depict a "decorated" military man in leather boots and velvet coat and a Chinese man with his long queue over his shoulder.

Lafe took his own life in the 1920s, and Annie's son preceded her in death. Her quilt was inherited by a niece, who passed it on to a friend who ran the hotel where Annie lived in her last years. The friend cared for Annie until her death.

Crazy Quilt

The intricate gold stitches that outline each elaborate Victorian Crazy quilt block tell us something of the importance of this work to its maker. The quilt surface is rich with embroidery, hand-painting, ribbons, and brocades—together with a banjo-playing frog, spiders, kissing youths, Chinese characters, a pig, flowers, and dancing figures, each exquisitely executed. Quotations and sayings in gold embroidery fill out the blue border, and twisted gold-satin braid outlines the binding.

Eliza Whetton Eliot, the wife of a banker in Milwaukee, Wisconsin, created this quilt as she anticipated the arrival of her last baby, a son born in 1883. The initials of Charles Eliot and his year of birth are stitched into the center block. It is believed that Eliza was born about 1840; she would have been forty-three when her son, who was not to survive his teenage years, was born.

The present owner inherited the quilt from his grandmother, who received it from her mother, a sister of the ill-fated Charles. He brought the quilt to California in the 1940s when he traveled on the Overland Limited Railway Train to attend Stanford University.

Eliza Whetton Eliot, who so abundantly embroidered the details of her Crazy quilt. c. 1880.

Feathered Star Variation with Garden Maze Set

When Mary Elizabeth Bowman Hylton Clapper boarded a train in Kansas in 1907 or 1908, she was headed for Lindsay, California. She brought with her this sparkling Feathered Star quilt, which she had completed years earlier.

Born in Johnson City, Tennessee, in 1852, and married to Elijah W. Hylton in the late 1870s, she made this quilt in her home in Virginia, where her husband farmed. She had two children before she was widowed. When she remarried, to a Mr. Clapper, they moved to Kansas, where he also farmed, and then to central California, where Mary's son was already living.

Quilted in diagonal and curved lines, this intricately pieced quilt is bold and dramatic. Mary added the binding, using her new hand-crank sewing machine.

The quilt passed from the maker to her daughter. The present owner, a great-granddaughter of the maker, received it from an aunt on the occasion of her marriage in 1972.

Blazing Star

Addie Beebe was born to pioneer parents in 1868 in Washington, Oregon (a town that no longer exists). Her father had cousins living in California, so when Addie was small, the family moved there, established a ranch, and raised grain. In 1889, Addie married Mr. Simms, and it was while living in her new home on their ranch near Cedarville that Addie pieced this top. It remained unfinished for many years. Addie had five children, one of whom died of chicken pox as an infant. Her daughter, Effie May Simms Hays, finished the quilt in the 1930s with the help of both her mother and her mother-in-law.

Effie, mother of three, "quilted a lot" with whatever she had. She cut her patterns from cardboard, then glued sandpaper on the back. Addie was a midwife in the

Mary Elizabeth Bowman Hylton Clapper, who brought her Feathered Star west from Virginia. c. 1905.

Crazy Crib Quilt, 1883, made in
Wisconsin. 60″ x 40″. Quiltmaker:
Eliza Whetton Eliot (1840?–1910?).
Details included. Collection of
Jared F. Boyd.

Feathered Star Variation with Garden Maze Set, family name: Snowflake Quilt, 1875–1890, made in Virginia. 77″ x 77″. Quiltmaker: Mary Elizabeth Bowman Hylton Clapper (1852–1934). Collection of Ann Perkins and Carolyn Matthews.

Blazing Star, 1880–1900 (quilted in 1930s), made in California. 58″ x 76″. Quiltmakers: Addie Beebe Simms (1868–1951?) and Effie May Simms Hays (1892–1984). Collection of Suzie Miller.

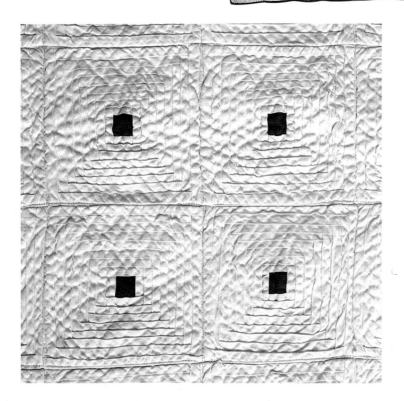

Log Cabin, Courthouse Steps, family name: Grandma Anderson's Log Cabin Quilt, 1880–1900, made in Canada. 67″ x 80″. Quiltmaker: Mary Cassady Anderson (1835–1928). Detail included. Collection of Ruth P. Ashton and Margaret A. Bowman.

early 1900s, when doctors were often scarce in the valley. A friend and neighbor, also a midwife, alternated with her: one watched all their children while the other helped in deliveries or did home nursing.

The present owner of the quilt is the great-granddaughter of the quiltmaker.

Log Cabin: Courthouse Steps Design

When Ruth Plumstead traveled from New York to California by train in 1924, she brought with her a quilt made by her grandmother. "This [quilt] has always symbolized 'home' to those who moved to California...it was made in the house on the family farm."[58]

In 1835, Ruth's grandmother, Mary Cassady, was born near Paris, Ontario, in Canada, where her family had lived for several generations. Nineteen years later she married farmer and auctioneer Daniel A. Anderson and gave birth to seven children, six of whom survived. This is her only known quilt. According to family history, Mary did her piecing while sitting at the bedside of her dying husband about 1889.

Mary's quilt passed to her daughter Adah, and it was Adah's daughter, Ruth, who brought it across the country to California. It is presently owned by Ruth and her daughter.

Press-laid, narrow, all-white fabric strips create a subtle relief pattern that contrasts with the bright red squares that reputedly symbolize the hearth at the center of the log cabin. A machine-stitched line at the edge of each block secures the layers in this striking Log Cabin quilt.

Mary Cassady Anderson, quilt-maker, pictured in the yard of the family farm in New York. c. 1915.

Old Maid's Puzzle

The 1850 census of Nantucket, Massachusetts, lists Mary Worth as head of her household, with two sons, aged fourteen and eleven. She had been widowed ten years earlier when her husband, Reuben B. Worth, a sea captain, died of consumption at age forty. Born to Sally and Charles Alley in 1805, Mary had wed at twenty-nine and become a widow just five years later. Her older son, Charles Albert, was then three years old, and her second son was born seven months after her husband's death. Mary never remarried.

Her son Charles left Massachusetts in the early 1850s, at about age fourteen, to sail as a cabin boy to California. He headed for the gold mines, but his career was cut short when everything belonging to him was stolen. He moved to San Francisco, where he eventually bought horses and a wagon and started the C. A. Worth Drayage Company. The business would grow into a trucking firm in the 1900s. In San Francisco, Charles married Winnie Coffin, who also came from Nantucket, and was probably a longtime acquaintance of the family. Mary joined Charles and Winnie in San Francisco during the 1850s. Reuben, Jr., Mary's second son, must have come to California about the same time. Only two years after their marriage, Reuben's wife, Ella F. Smith, died in San Francisco at the age of twenty-one.

Mary's fabrics, including shirtings and prints from the 1870s and 1880s, were selected to reflect a keen interest in outdoor life. Pieces are cut to feature the images of horses' heads, riding crops, horseshoes, dogs' heads, playing cards, a bee (or wasp), and the Epsom Derby. Several different shadings of a single print suggest she may have used salesman's samples.

The tied bedcover is two-sided, the back side appearing to make a more direct use of rectangular samples in its Hit and Miss pattern. The rich and varied brown prints alternate with light prints, and there is a center medallion of nine stars.

Mary made a second and smaller quilt that is also two-sided; it may have been a crib or doll quilt. Known as "Ma" Worth to her family, she always wore a long black dress with a white apron and a white cap.

The Victorian parlor of the home in which Mary Worth spent her last years. Pictured are two of her granddaughters, Eva and Mable Worth. 1884–1886.

Front: Old-Maid's Puzzle: *Back:* Hit and Miss with Medallion Center of Variable Stars. 1880–1900, made in California. 73″ x 73″. Quiltmaker: Mary Worth (1814–1906). Collection of Pat L. Nickols.

Irish Chain Variation, family name: The Red and White Quilt, 1880–1900 (quilted in 1942), made in Ohio. 83″ x 85″. Quiltmaker: Margaret Anthony Hall (1826–1904). Collection of Robert A. and Kathryn Hesser Weatherup.

When a great-great-granddaughter of Mary's received this quilt from an elderly cousin, she placed it in an antiques shop for sale. The present owner purchased the quilt and has pursued its history.

Irish Chain Variation

Margaret was one of seven children born to David Anthony "and wife," who moved from Jackson to Allen County, Ohio, and there spent their first year living in the old council house of the Shawnee Indians. Margaret went to work at the home of the Halls, to help when Grandmother Hall was ill. The Halls had moved to that area in 1835, and it was in their home that Margaret met Jesse, one of the six Hall children. Margaret and Jesse married in 1847.

Jesse was a farmer and, later, a soldier in the Civil War. In a family journal, written in 1937 by Margaret's son, is a description of how his parents built their first home:

> They cleared an opening in the woods, and my father, being somewhat of
> a carpenter and handy with tools, felled trees, scored, hewed and notched
> them, and in due time reared his log house. He rived his own shingles with
> rive and drawing knife.... In this log house were born...[six children].
> My father then decided it was time to build a larger and better house for
> his growing family. He prepared the wood and built a brick kiln and
> burned his own brick.[59]

After moving into her new house, Margaret gave birth to three more children. Two died at the age of four. Hall says, "I can see my mother yet as she sat with the old family Bible in her lap and turned to the two little curls cut from the locks of Estella and Angeline, and wept as she caressed them."[60]

After Jesse died and their children were grown, Margaret lived with her daughter Sarah Cass Hesser (Kate). Kate's husband and father-in-law owned a dry-goods store, and Margaret's various red prints reportedly came from the store's fabric samples. (She made a second quilt using blue samples.) In her last years, Margaret completed nine quilt tops. Her obituary offers some insight as to why she made few quilts until then.

> Her life was an unassuming one, most appreciated by those who knew her
> best. Her doors were always open to the poor and helpless, and especially
> did her heart go out to homeless orphans. She cared for as many as eight
> in her home for months at one time besides her own family. The young
> people to whom she gave a home at different times in her life, it would
> be impossible to enumerate. Teachers, ministers, relatives and strangers
> found a welcome at her hands. She was an ideal mother, devoted to a
> fault, yet rigid in discipline.[61]

The Quilt Circle of the First Methodist Episcopal Church in Redlands, California, quilted two of Margaret's remaining pieced tops in 1942. The Quilt Circle accepted contributions to the church as payment for their quilting.

In her Irish Chain, Margaret's precise hand-piecing is set off with a quilted pattern of hanging diamonds. The edge is finished with an applied facing on the third border.

Six of Margaret's quilt tops went to her granddaughters, and the others stayed in her daughter Kate's family. In 1920 the Hessers moved to California. Kate's husband and son came by car; Kate, her daughter-in-law, her granddaughters, and the quilts came by train.

Starburst

California Gibson was treasurer of Colusa County, California, for sixteen years. When she died in 1958, she left among her treasured possessions a Sunburst quilt

Starburst, family name: Sunburst,
1880–1900, made in California. 74″
x 80″. Quiltmaker: Sarah Frances
Larch Gibson (1852–1922). Collection of Teresa L. Thompson.

made by her mother, Sarah Gibson. California's father, Joseph Sitlem Gibson, had come to the gold fields with his cousins by wagon train from Missouri in 1850. He was about twenty-five and had little or no luck prospecting, so he turned instead to raising wheat for the bread the miners would surely need.

Sarah Francis Larch, born in Missouri in 1852, came as a young girl to Colusa to visit her sister. At a party in her honor, she met Joseph, twenty-seven years her senior. After her visit, she returned to her family in Missouri; Joseph followed her back to his home state and the two were married in Callaway County in 1874. They returned by train to California, where they built the large house near Williams, which still stands and is of local historical interest.

Married at twenty-two, Sarah spent her remaining life on that ranch, where she raised three children. After she was widowed, her eldest son and his family lived with her in the large family home. A family geneology documents that she was a great-great-granddaughter of Daniel Boone, tracing the line through Larch, Davis, and Hayes to Boone.

Sarah's mother had passed on her quilts and her knowledge of quilting to her daughter. Those quilts were worn out with use, but Sarah kept the tradition alive by making quilts for her own family, using the skills she had acquired as a teenager. Her quilting frame was set over chairs in an extra bedroom. An unusual collection of subtle browns, grays, and pinks in the diamonds was hand-pieced by Sarah for this radiating design. Checkered fabrics and printed patterns made the surface vibrant and alive. The overall quilting pattern is of parallel lines, finished with a narrow binding.

Sarah helped raise the two grandchildren who were living in her home, one of whom still has several of her quilts. This Starburst passed from Sarah to her daughter, Narra California (who was called Narra as a child and later by her middle name). After California's death, the quilt went to her niece, Rebecca, who gave it to "a very dear friend," the grandmother of the present owner.

Pinwheel Doll Quilt

In 1936, when Harriet Houston was seven years old, she received a doll quilt in the mail from her great-aunt Bertha Eldora Osborn. A letter to Harriet's mother from Bertha included this: "...also, glad she can use her doll quilt. I pieced that when I was not older than she is now."[62]

Bertha was seven in 1891 at the time she stitched this Pinwheel. Born near Jamesport, Missouri, she received music education in Braymer, Missouri, and at the Kansas City Conservatory. For thirty-five years she served as pianist for the First Baptist Church in Gilman City, Missouri. She never married, but lived with a married sister at whose home she completed many quilts.

Bertha's niece (Harriet's mother) had come by train to Yreka, California, in the early 1920s to visit relatives, and then to attend Chico Normal School at the Bidwell Mansion. After tonsilitis forced her to drop out of school, she returned to Yreka, married, and gave birth to her daughter Harriet, who received this quilt made by her great aunt. It still belongs to Harriet.

Baby Basket

Near the end of the Civil War, in 1865, Nancy Elizabeth Lamb was born in Macon County, Missouri. Her parents were farmers, and they moved from Missouri to South Dakota, back to Missouri, and on to Oklahoma. Nancy's mother sewed for all members of the family, making suits and work clothes for her husband and sons, dresses for the girls, and all the family bedding. She related that as a girl she had made (by hand) all her brothers' overalls. "Every worn-out garment had one 'good'

Pinwheel Doll Quilt, 1890–1895, made in Missouri. 18″ x 18″. Quiltmaker: Bertha Eldora Osborn (1884–1958). Collection of Harriet D. Houston.

Baby Basket, 1880–1910 (quilted 1910 or after), made in Oklahoma. 62″ x 77″. Quiltmaker: Nancy Elizabeth Lamb Holmes (1865–1932). Collection of Leona Galley.

spot where she could salvage a piece or two for the cover [quilt] she was working on at that time."[63]

At age twenty-three, Nancy married farmer Frank Holmes, who had come to America from Stanton, England. They had eight children, three of whom died before their second birthdays.

Around 1910, the Holmeses moved to California and bought a chicken farm outside Sebastopol. There, Nancy finished this quilt, probably pieced and assembled much earlier in Oklahoma. Caring for her large family and helping with the family farm must have left little time for quilting, but when she moved to Ardin in Modoc County, she lived in town. She then had both a quilting frame and a sewing machine. Remembering pieces of conversations through the years, Nancy's granddaughter recalls that, even with four children under the age of fifteen at home, "[her] grandmother probably had some leisure for the first time in her married life."

The pieced baskets have handles added in blind-stitch appliqué and are quilted in a fan pattern, with several different borders. The quilt now belongs to Nancy's granddaughter, who also has many of her grandmother's pieced tops.

Nancy Elizabeth Lamb Holmes with her family on the day of her daughter's wedding. Pictured from top left, Joe Oliver, Beaulah May (wearing the dress her mother made for her wedding), Virgie Louise, and in the front row, Nancy's husband Frank Holmes, Ralph Lee, the baby Winnie Belle, and Nancy. Missouri, 1907.

Red Work

Embroidered in bright red outline stitch on white, an inscription on this Red Work quilt reads:

*Made by
Mrs. John Willis
Tully, N.Y.
For Her Grand daughter*

Few details are known of Grandmother Hannah Willis's life. She was widowed when John Willis died in 1888. Her daughter, Ada Belle, born in 1866, was married and soon widowed. In 1892, at twenty-six, Ada married her second husband, thirty-eight-year-old James T. Irwin, a salt-well driller in New York. His ill health prompted their move to a better climate, and in 1901, Ada and James arrived in Pomona, California. With them on the westbound train was their six-year-old daughter Evelyn and the quilt that documented her birth. Inscribed on the quilt were Evelyn's birth date (October 4, 1895), birth weight (8⅓ pounds), and name, together with the names of both her parents and her grandmother, the quilt's maker. The lettering for the embroidery had been inscribed on the fabric by Evelyn's father.

Among the quilt's more formal designs, reminiscent of illustrations from that time, are some that must have had personal significance: a pumpkin, the flag, a potato, and a cradle. According to family recollections, other drawings were taken from Evelyn's storybooks.

A boat, *The Little Evelyn*, which is depicted on the quilt, is believed to have belonged to a cousin who named it for the baby. A note attached to the quilt when it was inherited by the present owner, the quilter's great-granddaughter, states that it won a first prize in the 1899 New York State Fair. Quotations in red outline stitch on the cotton fabric came from a variety of sources, including Shakespeare and the Bible. All, including the following, refer to sleep, nighttime, or dawn:

*Happy the man that when the day is done
Lies down to sleep with nothing of regret*

*Count that day lost
Whose lone descending sun
Sees from thy hand no
Worthy Actions done*

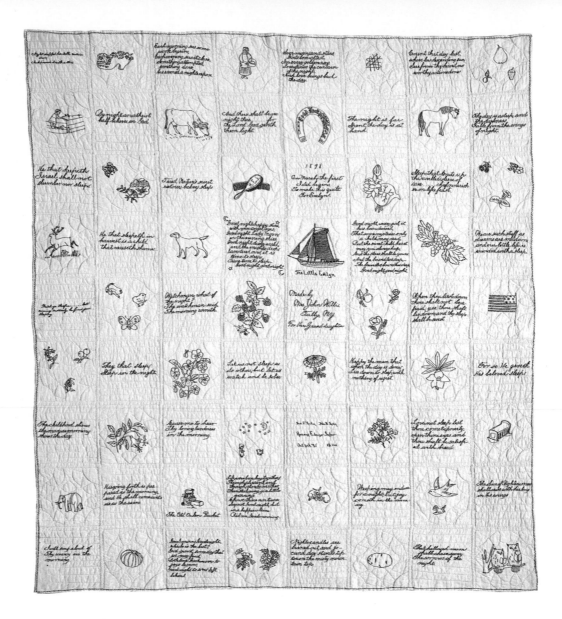

Red Work, Embroidered Birth Announcement Quilt, 1898, made in New York. 64″ x 73″. Quiltmaker: Hannah Willis (1840–?). Detail included. Collection of Evelyn Adair Banta Juras.

School House, Houses, family name: Little Red Schoolhouse, 1890–1910, made in Tennessee. 83″ x 65″. Quiltmaker: Reverend Jesse Crosswhite (1826–1891). Collection of Alberta B. Davis.

Double Irish Chain, 1890–1910 (quilted in 1927), made in New Jersey. 69″ x 92″. Quiltmakers: Julie Pinkney Osborne (1846–1939) and Rosabel Osborne Schefcik (1886–1975). Collection of Julie A. Marvel.

The quotations are not only a keen reflection of Victorian sentiment but also were this grandmother's means of offering moral direction to the little girl.

Quilted lines parallel the seams of the pieced blocks. In the quotation blocks, horizontal lines accentuate lettering and a pattern of fan stitching covers the pictorial areas. The fabric is turned to the back with a line of feather stitching at the edge.

School House

The Reverend Jesse Crosswhite was not only a minister and a schoolteacher but also a quiltmaker. He was born in Tennessee in 1826, where he married Lavinia Thomas and raised their eight children. A family history relates that he made this quilt during the Civil War, when he was actively involved in the Underground Railroad. Some of the fabrics and the pattern itself, however, suggest a late-nineteenth-century date. The quilt blocks may have been made at one time and assembled with the sashing later. The houses were hand-pieced and tied while the binding was added by machine-stitching.

The quilt is currently in the possession of the quiltmaker's great-granddaughter, who says, "[The quilt] is the only thing I have of my great-grandfather's. I remember seeing this on my grandmother's bed as I was growing up. I am seventy-five years old...."

This tied quilt was given to Rhoda Crosswhite Simpson, a schoolteacher, the fifth of Jesse's eight children. Rhoda and her husband, who was a pharmacist at a St. Louis hotel, moved to California in 1902 and brought the quilt with them. They settled in Los Angeles with a son and teenaged twin daughters. Family history relates that Rhoda's husband died soon after their arrival, and Rhoda became a writer. In addition to her books, she worked as a screenwriter, as did her son. A scenario writer for D. W. Griffith, Rhoda's son became the first screenwriter to have his name appear in a motion picture's credits.

Double Irish Chain

Using a saucer for her pattern, Rosabel Osborne Schefcik traced circles onto the white squares of fabric in her Double Irish Chain quilt top. Then, she and her mother, Julia Pinkney Osborne, who had taught her to sew, quilted it in the living room of their Oakland apartment.

Julie Pinkney Osborne, at left, and her daughter, Rosabel Osborne Schefcik, quilting on their Double Irish Chain. Oakland, California, 1927.

Married to a farmer, Julia had given birth to seven children, four of whom died in infancy. It was when her husband retired that they came to California, around 1923, driving across the country from New Jersey. Their daughter Rosabel, at age twenty, had married Joseph Frank Schefcik, a pharmacist, and they lived in Asbury Park, New Jersey. Along with their own fifteen-year-old daughter, Joseph and Rosabel accompanied the Osbornes on the long trip to the West Coast. This quilt is believed to have been pieced in New Jersey and brought to California, where it was quilted in 1927.

In 1934, Rosabel was widowed. She was a seamstress all her life and used the scraps she accumulated while sewing for others to make many of her quilts. While living in Oakland, she started each morning by taking her sewing machine and tools to one of the homes where she did dressmaking. The family believes it was during the 1930s that she did alterations for the I. Magnin store, working there six days a week. On Saturdays, employees were expected to go home for dinner and return to work for the rest of the evening. It was Rosabel who announced one Saturday that she wasn't coming back after dinner; she was going to spend time with her family. According to the story, her refusal was instrumental in initiating the policy that eliminated Saturday night work. Rosabel continued her work as a seamstress up into her seventies.

The Irish Chain top was quilted in overlapping circles and crosshatch pattern, and was finished in 1927. It passed from mother to daughter and is presently owned by Rosabel's granddaughter, Julia's great-granddaughter.

Cigar Ribbon

When the Nevada County Children's Society held a fund-raiser quilt show in 1980, this quilt was donated by the daughter of the woman who made it. Born in Seneca, Missouri, around 1870, quiltmaker Maude Lillian Riley came to California as a child with her mother and father, and attended private schools in Healdsburg and Santa Rosa. In 1892, she married banker and businessman Charles Sumner Beach in San Jose.

Maude had one daughter, Rofena, who graduated from Stanford and taught in the Oakland public schools. Rofena married in 1932 and now, at ninety-three, recalls that her "father used to order his cigars direct from Havana; they came packed in wooden boxes with the cigars in bundles of four or six fastened with silk ribbons. Most were yellow."[64] She remembers that her mother was overjoyed when some arrived in other brilliant colors. According to Dorothy Cozart, the different colors of ribbons were used to designate the various grades of cigars."[65]

In Maude's quilt the yellows are arranged in gradations and all the extra lettering was reserved for the border. Maude made this quilt for herself, and she must have enjoyed some of the various labels: Girl From Paris, Society Manners, Public Speaker, Renown, Sublimes, Tolstoy, Victor Hugo, and Nathan Hale. Charles must have enjoyed many hours of puffing.

Maude embellished the silk and satin ribbons with embroidery stitches over each seam line. The current owner purchased the quilt at the 1980 fund-raiser.

In 1979, a quilter wrote to a California newspaper for information about her cigar-ribbon pillowslip, which included several of the same brands identified in this quilt. The answer read as follows:

> While such a pillowslip makes a great conversation piece and keepsake, John McLaughlin, vice president in charge of marketing for the General Cigar Company in New York, told us cigar wrappers always have been printed on paper to his knowledge. "White Owl, which we manufacture, never has been printed on anything but paper," he said. . . .He suggested that perhaps someone went to a great deal of trouble to silk screen the labels for the pillowslip.[66]

It seems remarkable that the popular cigar silks of the late 1800s and early 1900s were unknown to a representative within the tobacco industry. Almost every quilter is familiar with the printed silks used with such zeal and ingenuity by late-Victorian quiltmakers.

Double Nine-Patch Variation

Eleven-year-old Dessa Eliza Jepson, living in Sespe Canyon, California, started a quilt that was to be for her doll. Six years later, when her mother died, Dessa began studies to become a teacher and, at the same time, kept house for her father, who told her she couldn't marry until her quilt was finished. For years, the top grew and grew.

In 1924, at age thirty-six, Dessa married William Salon Keatley, a cowboy and oil-field worker. They had three daughters, and one recalls:

> When we were children, our mother would take out the quilt and point out different materials and where they originated. I remember dark prints

A *printed cigar silk bearing the company name secures a half-wheel of cigars. Reproduced from* Le Livre du Connoisseur de Cigare *by Robert Laffont, Paris, 1967.*

This cigar-box label shows the cigars bundled and tied. Reproduced from Smokers, Segars and Stickers *by A. D. Faber, New York, 1949.*

Cigar Ribbon Quilt, 1890–1910, made in California. 59″ x 72″. Quiltmaker: Maude Lillian Riley Beach (1870–1950 ?). Detail included. Collection of Joan T. Guenther.

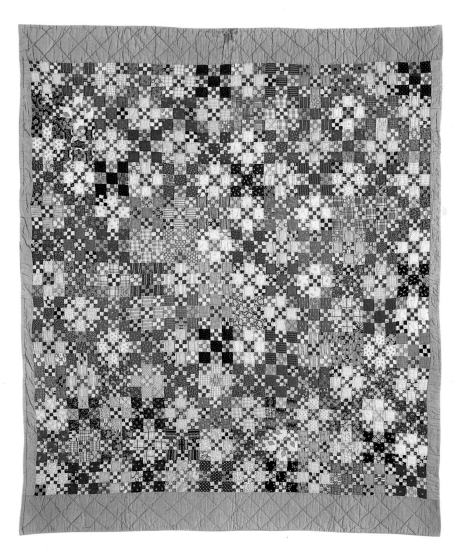

Double Nine-Patch Variation, family name: The Doll Quilt That Got Away, 1890–1910 (quilted in the 1920s), made in California. 68″ x 82″. Quiltmaker: Dessa Eliza Jepson Keatley (1888–1984). Collection of Elisabeth E. Basore.

Crazy Quilt with Fan Variation and Stars, 1890–1915, made in Pennsylvania. 63″ x 63″. Quiltmaker unknown. Collection of Barbara K. Raker.

that were dresses of *her* mother's...and one square from a shirt belonging to the clerk of the school board where our mother first taught.[67]

Years after piecing this top, Dessa quilted it with a group from her church. One of Dessa's daughters, a writer, based her latest novel, *And Condors Danced*, on the stories told by her mother about life in Sespe Canyon.

This Double Nine Patch presently belongs to a daughter of the quiltmaker. The multicolored cotton fabrics are quilted in outline stitching and crosshatching.

Crazy Quilt with Fan Variation

From Harrisburg, Pennsylvania, the passengers in the 1919 Cole Touring Sedan headed across the country and through the South Dakota badlands. Complete with side-tire mounts and curtains, the car was fitted with two quilts on the inside to keep the passengers warm. The drive required three months, and eventually took the family down the coast of California to Santa Monica.

Ralph C. Kirk, his wife, Helen, and their six-year-old son made the trip in the summer of 1922. Ralph, a writer for periodicals (among them *The Saturday Evening Post*), collected story information and wrote while on the trip. A daughter was born a few months after their arrival in California.

Although this Fan quilt was made just five to twenty-five years before the Kirks' departure, no recollections reveal its origins. Who made it, why, and how it came to travel with them are unknown.

Embroidered Block Fund-raiser Quilt

A group of women working with the Vincent Methodist Episcopal Church Building Fund in Los Angeles embroidered this Fund-raiser quilt. Traditionally, Fund-raiser quilts include the names of supporters who contribute money in exchange for the privilege of being identified on the work. Here, over six hundred names are embroidered, each one a part of an organized pattern of names within a block. Each block contains an image of some living thing—bird, flower, dog, cat, mollusk, or leaf—and a unique arrangement of the names, one of which appears in Chinese characters.

A large central block depicts the church, underneath which is written "Los Angeles, 1904." Also listed are its architect, pastor, official board, and building committee.

The machine-quilted lines are used to reinforce the blocks and run parallel to the seams. The back is finished, although it has no filler and no overall quilting pattern. The present owners purchased this Red Work quilt in an antiques shop.

Crazy Star

In 1878, thirty-year-old Eunice Catherine Vestal wed Joseph Robinett in Pleasant Grove, California. During this, the second of her three marriages, she gave birth to her only child, Sarah Addie. When Sarah was eighteen, she married, and it was when Sarah's daughter was born that Eunice combined flannel, wool, twill, and velveteen with prints and checks in this Crazy Star quilt for granddaughter Elsie Bernice Davis. She then embroidered its surface, unifying the star and border by adding an unusual linear pattern that meanders through the background.

Eunice made many quilts that have survived; among them is her earliest-known work, bearing her sister's name and an embroidered date, 1868. Eunice would have been twenty. When she was widowed after her third marriage, Eunice moved into her daughter's home.

Elsie treasured this Birthday quilt, and kept it, along with other handmade items, wrapped and tied in cloth sugar bags in a cedar chest. Upon Elsie's death, her two

Eunice Catherine Jones, on the left in the back seat, is pictured with her daughter's family with whom she spent her last years after being widowed for the third time. At the left is Jabes Griffith Davis, her son-in-law; Sarah Addie Davis, her daughter; and granddaughter, Elsie Davis (for whom Eunice made this quilt). The woman seated next to Eunice is believed to be Jabes's sister, and the children on horseback are unidentified. Photographed on the farm near Pleasant Grove, California, 1909.

Red Work, Embroidered Block Fund-raiser Quilt, 1904, made in California. 82″ x 85″. Quiltmaker: the Vincent Methodist Episcopal Church Building Fund Group. Detail included. Collection of Mary Jane and Sally Van Natta.

Crazy Star, 1906, made in California. 68″ x 78″. Quiltmaker: Eunice Catherine Vestal Mobray Robinett Jones (1848–1929). Collection of Bernice M. Harreld.

Oak Leaf and Reel, 1900–1914, made in Nebraska. 69″ x 71″. Quiltmaker: Eliza Jane Leonard (1833–1927). Collection of Lois Ream Goodwill.

daughters found the cedar chest and a doll trunk, and when her sister chose the doll trunk, the present owner inherited the cedar chest containing her great-grandmother's quilt.

Oak Leaf and Reel

When Eliza Jane Leonard was eighty-one, she finished this quilt for the 1914 wedding of her granddaughter, who never used it and remembers, "It had never been washed. It still had a spot of grandma's blood on it."

Eliza was born in 1833 in Ohio, and was married to Alvin Leonard; little else is known about her or her quilt. According to a family recollection, Eliza purchased her fabric at the Homer, Nebraska, Country Grocery and Mercantile Store for nineteen cents a yard.

Eliza's daughter Emma, widowed and with five small children to support, made rag rugs on a loom and delivered mail by horse and buggy. Emma's own daughter, Harriet, endured the dust storms and drought that devastated Nebraska in the 1930s and then followed other relatives to California around 1938. The quilt, given to Harriet as a wedding present, accompanied her in the car on the trip west. She later gave the quilt to her niece.

The crisp freshness of this quilt is evidence of the special care it has been given. Sashings are quilted with a cable pattern, and the background is crosshatched. Outline quilting emphasizes the blind-stitch appliqué. The current owner says, "It was made by my great-grandmother...the only heirloom I own."

Darting Minnow and the Albert Quilt

The Hurd family came to America in 1639 and settled in Woodbury, Connecticut, where a family home built in 1680 still stands. The family later moved to Vermont and then to Pennsylvania. It was in Springborough, Pennsylvania, that Harriet Newel Hurd, the sixth of nine children, was born in 1829. Her father, Isaac Hurd, was a sawmill owner, hotel keeper, and farmer.

Living on a nearby farm was the Thomas family, where Samuel Johnson Thomas was the eldest of ten children. Samuel's father, Elijah, strictly enforced the Pennsylvania law that decreed a son's labors belong to the father until the son reaches the age of twenty-one. So, intent on a law career, Samuel spent the days teaching school and working on the farm; at night he propped his books on the mantel and read standing up to keep from falling asleep.

In 1855, Samuel passed the bar and became a circuit judge in Kansas, traveling on horseback through the countryside to hold court where needed. Harriet came to Topeka, where she and Samuel were married and established their home. A son, Mark Augustus, was born a year later, and family history suggests that he was the first white child born in Kansas.

In the late 1850s, both a drought and a grasshopper invasion devastated the area. Utterly discouraged, the Thomases returned to Conneauville, Pennsylvania, where a daughter was born. Samuel practiced law until the beginning of the Civil War, when he served as a captain in the Union Army with Colonel Curtin.

Harriet was widowed when Samuel died at age thirty-nine. *A History of a Thomas Family* attributes his death to tuberculosis and a kick by a horse; perhaps both were contributing factors.

Harriet raised their two children in Pennsylvania, where both were educated through a provision in Samuel's will. Mark graduated from college, became a justice of the peace, and married. He later took a job as a corporation secretary in San Francisco. His sister, Minnie, graduated from the Boston Conservatory of Music.

For the celebration of her son's thirtieth wedding anniversary, Harriet made this special Darting Minnow quilt. It includes her own birth date, her son's anniversary

Eliza Jane Leonard is shown with members of her family. On the far left is granddaughter, Harriet Glissman, who received the Oak Leaf and Reel quilt as a wedding present in 1914. It now belongs to the child pictured on the left who has her finger in her mouth. Eliza is seated in front. 1927.

Harriet Hurd Thomas is shown in front of the family home in Conneautville, Pennsylvania, where she spent her later years living with her mother. The young woman on the right is unidentified, but she may be Harriet's daughter who, when widowed many years later, moved back to this house to live with Harriet.

Darting Minnow, 1909, made in
Pennsylvania. 76″ x 74½″. Quilt-
maker: Harriet Newel Hurd
Thomas (1829–1927). Collection of
Mr. and Mrs. J. A. Thomas, Jr.

The Albert Quilt, with Stars and
Stripes, 1917, made in Pennsyl-
vania. 29½″ x 41½″. Quiltmaker:
Harriet Newel Hurd Thomas
(1829–1927). Collection of Mr. and
Mrs. J. A. Thomas, Jr.

My Beloved Flag, family name: Hawaiian Flag Quilt, 1900–1920, made in Hawaii. 71″ x 71″. Quiltmaker unknown. Collection of Bernice Steinmetz Brown.

New York Beauty Variation, 1900–1920, made in California. 80″ x 96″. Quiltmaker: Hannah Elizabeth Wilder Raglin (1867–1954). Detail included. Collection of Loren Raglin.

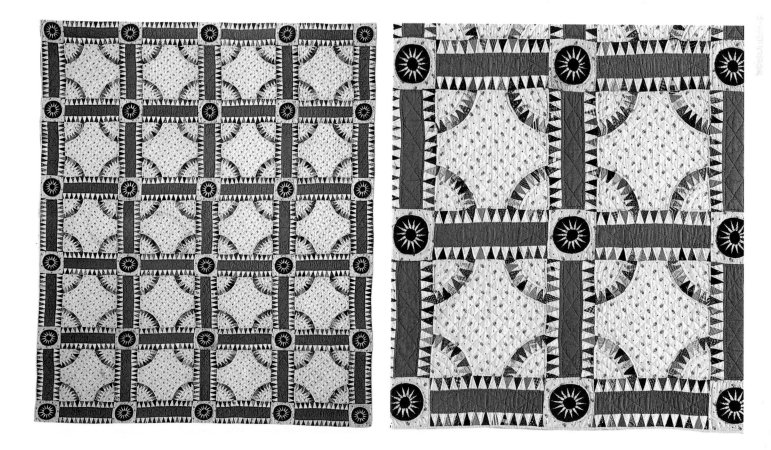

date and his name (Mark A.), her daughter-in-law's name (Jennie), and the last name they all shared. Quilted between the dates are birds and the inscription "Mother." Harriet was eighty when the quilt was completed and she sent it to San Francisco.

Eight years later, Harriet made a quilt for her great-grandson, Johnson Albert Thomas, Jr. Pieced into the Albert Quilt in blue and white are the dates of her birth (1829) and his fourth birthday (1917). Thirteen stars are appliquéd to the front, and a boldly striped backing completes the patriotic theme. This quilt was also entrusted to the U.S. mails and sent on its way.

Harriet moved into the old family home and stayed there with her mother for many years, during the latter's remaining lifetime. After her mother's death, Harriet remained, and her then widowed daughter, Minnie, came to live with her.

My Beloved Flag

Most quilts brought into California came from the East. Open spaces and opportunity were westward, and as immigrants arrived, households were set up and quilts emerged from trunks and boxes. Only occasionally did quilts move in the opposite direction, as this one did. Made in Hawaii, it went east by ship to California.

When Blanche T. Fetter was married in Hawaii in 1921, she received a quilt as a wedding gift. Three more weddings followed as Blanche's sisters married, and to commemorate the ceremonies their mother purchased quilts from the local Hawaiian women who made them. This one was particularly prized, for it features the Hawaiian coat of arms.

In 1924, Blanche, her husband, and their two small children came to visit in Pacific Grove. They brought the quilt with them, and they never left the area.

King Kalahaua's coat of arms is depicted in the center of the quilt, surrounded by four flags. In each flag, the Union Jack is shown with seven stripes, representing the seven Hawaiian islands. The lettering, accomplished with reverse-appliqué work, reads "Ku'u hae Aloha," which means "My Beloved Flag," the name of this pattern. Tiny cross-stitches edge the appliqué. The unknown quiltmaker used parallel lines of quilting in the flags, in contrast to the echoing lines of the "Hawaiian quilting" in the central area.

The quilt now belongs to Blanche's daughter and serves as a poignant and vivid reminder of her mother's home state and heritage.

New York Beauty Variation

The Raglin and Wilder families were all from Missouri and were friends there before moving to California. Several marriages took place between the two families, including that of Hannah Elizabeth Wilder, born in Paskenta in 1867, to George Washington Raglin.

Hannah's education was minimal, but she was known to have read to her husband, who was probably illiterate. George was a laborer in 1880 and later raised sheep. He also owned a hay baler and went from ranch to ranch baling hay during the season. "Hannah cooked for the hands...the men worked in the fields and the women worked in the kitchen. They traveled from ranch to ranch as help was needed."[68]

The area around Paskenta, California, experienced extensive contact, and frequent conflicts, with local Maidu Indians, starting when the gold miners arrived by the hundreds in the middle 1800s. Although the family story that George's father was killed by the Maidu Indians and his children were then abducted and raised by them is unsubstantiated, court records do verify the marriages of several Raglin men to Maidu women.

Hannah started to quilt at about age twenty-five, having taught herself, and her

Hannah Elizabeth Raglin, maker of the New York Beauty, with her husband, George Washington Raglin.

first quilt was used by her husband as a horse blanket. She later made a quilt top for each of her five sons and a daughter. Although few of the tops were actually quilted, this New York Beauty was finished and kept by Hannah.

When she was widowed, Hannah went to live with a son in the Trinity Mountains. Found in her home after Hannah's death, the quilt now belongs to a grandson. It has crosshatch, outline, and diamond cable quilting combined to add further pattern to a quilt already full of action and vitality. A Butterfly quilt on which Hannah was working when she died was finished by her daughter-in-law and made into two quilts for Hannah's grandchildren.

Red Cross

To the varied reasons for which women made quilts—need, frugality, pleasure—wartime suggested another: patriotic expression. During World War I, this patriotic pursuit was encouraged by the Red Cross and through magazine articles.

> America's entry into the war fueled the quilt revival because the United States government actually urged its citizens to make quilts! In 1918, there appeared in numerous magazines and newspapers the slogan: "Make quilts—save the blankets for our boys over there."[69]

In 1917, *The Modern Priscilla* magazine featured an article giving directions, patterns, and procedures for Fund-raiser quilts. A sample ticket and receipt form was included, along with the suggestion of a twenty-five-cent fee per signature. The article states, "The idea is not complicated at all, and consists simply in selling squares or space to be inscribed with the name of the contributor."[70]

In 1918, Elsie Prewett Connable and her mother, Hannah Jane Prewett, embarked on the sewing of a Fund-raiser quilt. The 392 people who signed the quilt donated one dollar each to the Red Cross, and Elsie embroidered their names in red outline stitch. In the center of the quilt, the names of the men then in service were embroidered white on red. It was machine-quilted by Mary E. Bash, whose name is embroidered in the corner block along with the date and the Red Cross chapter. The quilt was intended for eventual sale, and Elsie's husband, Edwin H. Connable, paid one hundred dollars to the Red Cross to own it.

Elsie was born in Gallatin, Missouri, and attended college in Bethany. She was married at twenty-six to Edwin, a farmer and cattleman. They lived in a large, two-story stone farmhouse, where Elsie set up her quilting frame in an extra room adjacent to the kitchen and dining room. Two hired girls made it possible for Elsie to find time to quilt. She made heavy paper patterns and worked alone unless her mother, who lived nearby, helped her.

In 1920, Edwin's health prompted their move to California. The quilt went with them and was later passed to the present owner, who is the daughter and granddaughter of the quiltmakers. Other quilts of Elsie's belong to her granddaughters.

Crazy Quilt with Appliqué

Lilly Anderson spent many hours in the Salvation Army store, where she collected woolen pants and jackets for her quilting. The discarded clothing provided her with good pieces of durable fabric, to which she added a few patches of velvet and bright-hued bits of appliqué in her Crazy patchwork. Several moons, leaves, a star, and a bell offer a striking contrast to the somber geometric pieces of her background fabrics. It is a touching and poignant effort to bring a little of the luxuriance of Victorian Crazy work to her utilitarian and practical bedcover.

Born in Crystal Lake (or Robbinsdale), Minnesota, in 1865, Lilly Ann Gibbs at sixteen married Robert Chase Anderson. Lilly gave birth to eleven children, two of whom died in infancy; all were born in the large white house that overlooked

Hannah Jane Prewett, who worked with her daughter, Elsie, to make the Red Cross quilt.

Elsie Prewett, pictured in 1905, just before her marriage to Edwin Hurst Connable.

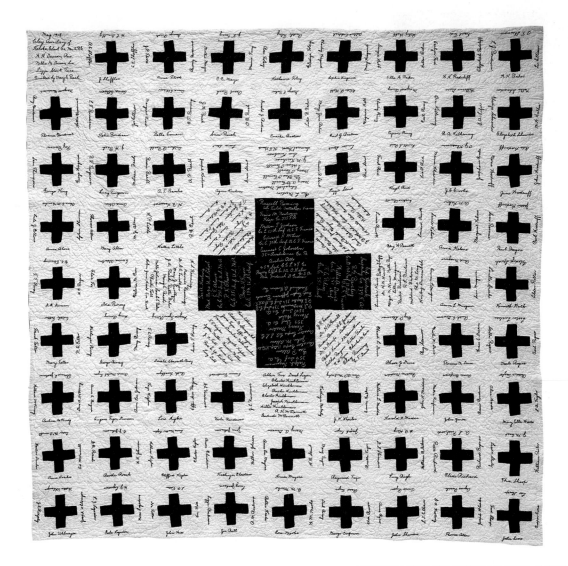

Red Cross Signature Quilt, 1918, made in Missouri. 78″ x 78″. Quiltmakers: Hannah Jane Prewett (1847–1933) and Elsie Prewett Connable (1879–1968). Detail included. Collection of Pauline Shattuck.

Crazy Quilt with Appliqué, family name: Grandma's Crazy Quilt, 1920, made in California. 65″ x 92″. Quiltmaker: Lily Ann Gibbs Anderson (1865–1922). Collection of Hazel Sawyer.

Crazy Quilt with Appliqué, family name: Friendship Name Quilt, 1920–1925, made in Mississippi. 74″ x 83″. Quiltmaker: Zella Flowers Roten (1889–1947). Collection of Sadie Roten Bartal.

Double Wedding Ring, family name: Gregg Family Quilt, 1920–1930, made in Texas. 71″ x 86″. Quiltmaker: Lorilla Gregg (1865–1934). Collection of Lee and Mary Staton.

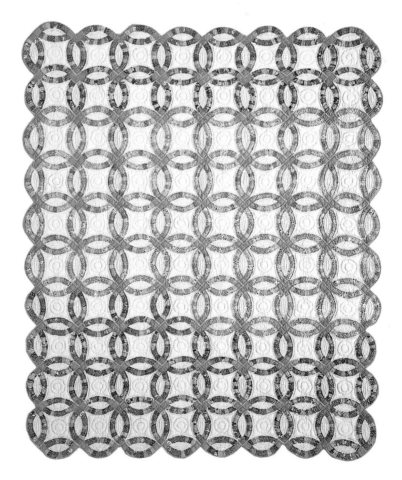

Lilly Ann Gibbs Anderson, who made the Crazy quilt with appliqué, and her husband, Robert Chase Anderson. 1914.

Crystal Lake. When the youngest child was still a toddler, the Andersons sold their house and, with Lilly's father and the children, traveled by train to California.

Robert was in poor health, and advertisements boasted that the move west was to the "only perfect climate in the world and the grandest scenery under the sun."[71] In the West, they traveled from place to place to keep Robert in warm weather, which seemed to ease his discomfort. A team of horses, with the hand-built wagon hitched behind, kept them moving up and down the state and into Oregon. A canvas cover protected the wagon when they bedded down at night.

The Andersons were migrant workers, finding jobs in fruit orchards, or vegetable fields, or canneries. As the family moved from Grass Valley, Marysville, Red Bluff, and Fresno, to Santa Cruz, they all worked at whatever jobs were available. They next went to Oregon, where Lilly's ability as a "crack shot" supplemented their staple of beans and fish with ducks and wild turkey. The family adopted an injured magpie, which they kept as a pet and taught to repeat words. Its vocabulary extended to "hello," "hungry," and "beans."

When Robert's health began to fail, they decided to drive their wagon to Phoenix. It was a long and difficult trip, much of it on foot to help save their horses as they hauled the heavy wagon over sand. They encountered dust storms and suffered a shortage of water and food. When they at last arrived in Phoenix, Robert went to work for the telephone company, and for seven hundred dollars, they bought a house with a barn for the horses and a chicken coop. They later bought a small ranch, and all the younger children entered school, all in the third grade, that being the level to which the mother had educated them as they traveled.

During World War I, when Lilly was in her fifties, the Salvation Army had a tremendous influx of wool socks, knitted by well-meaning women whose enthusiasm for warming soldiers' feet exceeded their skill with knitting needles. These socks came in a great variety of unwearable shapes and sizes. Lilly would undo the misproportioned sections and reknit them. At the end of World War I, Lilly's family moved back to Santa Cruz, where Lilly made a quilt for each of her daughters.

In Santa Cruz, Lilly and Robert were uniformed officers in the Salvation Army. They attended meetings regularly and spent many hours on street corners, singing and bringing "lost souls" into their ranks for salvation. (This probably accounts for the appliquéd hand bell on the quilt.) Two of their sons were to continue their parents' dedication to this work.

Lilly's wool quilt is embroidered with contrasting color at each pieced line. Short red stitches on the surface indicate where yarn was pulled through and tied on the back.

The present owner, a granddaughter of Lilly's, keeps the quilt wrapped in a cedar chest because it has become fragile. When she looks at it, she says she still wonders: "How did you manage? Raised nine children, with a sick husband, and constantly on the move..."[72]

Zella Flowers Roten with her daughter, Sadie, about 1915. A tied quilt is hung as a backdrop for this photograph.

Crazy Quilt with Appliqué

When Sadie Roten boarded a crowded train to California looking for work in 1943, she brought with her the quilt her mother, Zella Flowers Roten, had made with the help of Sadie and friends. Born in 1889 in Conway, Mississippi, Zella at nineteen had married Booker Roten, a thirty-five-year-old farmer. Their only child, Sadie, was born the next year.

In 1922 and 1923, Zella and teenaged Sadie assembled this top from embroidered blocks made by neighbors, friends, and relatives. Along with names and dates, the quilt's embroidered rabbits, cats, chickens, geese, and ducks mingle with stitched flowers and birds. "We swapped fabric back and forth and used scraps from my dresses," Sadie says. "We had a good time. We would invite friends in for a potluck, and you only got invited if you could quilt."[73]

In the summer they gardened and worked in the fields, where they picked cotton and corn. But in the winter they made quilts and "entertained" themselves. Quilting was done in the daytime, with good light; the coal-oil lamps used at night were inadequate for sewing.

> We made our own bats for the filling. Used cards, as we called them, to card the cotton. We took our patterns off old quilts, and cut them from cardboard. There were screws in the ceiling, and the old quilting frame was hung up there. We wound the quilt up and pulled it out of the way...[74]

It was when a friend went to San Francisco to see her husband, due back with the army, that Sadie made the trip. It was exciting, crowded, and seemingly endless. Once she and the quilt had arrived in San Francisco, Sadie got a job at Ingel's shipyard and became a welder. There she met Albert Bartal, an electrical foreman, whom she married. They had one son. Zella, who had been a widow since 1936, grieved continually after Sadie's departure, so Sadie and Albert brought her to San Francisco, where she spent two years with them before her accidental death in 1947. Zella's only grandson was born the following year. The quilt still belongs to Sadie Roten Bartal, and is among her most cherished possessions.

Double Wedding Ring

For Christmas 1930, in Santa Ana, California, Florence Staton received a box in the mail from Sulphur Bluff in northeast Texas. It contained this Double Wedding Ring quilt, made a few years earlier by Lorilla Gregg, who sent it to Florence. When Christmas 1934 arrived, Florence in turn gave the quilt to her son, Lee Staton, Jr., and his wife, Maude. The following letter accompanied the quilt:

> *To Lee and Maude.*
> *The sentiment and history of the quilt.*
> *This quilt was made by an old slave negro of your great grand Father Emanuel Samuel Gregg. Her name is Lorilla Gregg, taking the name from her husbands master. She selected the pattern and colors, pieced, set together, quilted and bound it, padded it with the cotton picked off of Jerrys farm. And Jerry is Carolines boy and Caroline was your great grand Mother Greggs slave-housekeeper. And Lorilla the one that made the quilt is Jerry's wife. She is seventy years old.*
> *This December twenty five*
> *Nineteen hundred and thirty four*
>   *from Dad and Mother Staton*

Caroline, the former slave of Samuel and Cinderella Gregg, lived in Sulphur Bluff, Texas, prior to the Civil War; she remained there afterward, living immediately adjacent to Cinderella, then a widow of fifty-one. The 1870 census for Hopkins County, Texas (Sulphur Bluff area), lists Caroline as female, black, age thirty, domestic servant, with children, including Jerry, age four. The census of a decade later shows them at the same address. Caroline's son Jerry married Lorilla Gregg, and they maintained a close relationship with Cinderella's descendant, exemplified by the gift of this quilt.

Maude and Lee Staton presented the quilt as a wedding present to their son and his wife in 1961. It is outline quilted, and additional circles are stitched into the white areas between the rings. The transition from light pastels to darker values at the ends is unique.

109

In the late 1870s, there was keen excitement among Pasadenans regarding an observatory to be built atop Mount Wilson. The trail up the mountain was an arduous one, with steep grades to the crest 5,800 feet above the basin. In 1889, the first of a series of telescopes was installed in an observatory in an area later cited for its "inaccessibility, lack of sufficient water and...overabundance of rattlesnakes."[75]

"Pasadenans fairly burst with pride and excitement at the prospect of their mountain becoming an astronomical center of the world,"[76] and a "Mount Wilson War" broke out over the rights of entrepreneurs eager to capitalize on the tourists who came to see the observatory.

To celebrate and honor the observatory that had been outfitted in 1917 with the one-hundred-inch Hooker telescope, the quiltmaker appliquéd representations of the two major structures of what was then the world's largest observatory, adding the moon and Saturn to the quilt's nearly one hundred stars. The large stars form the Big Dipper, although the heavens had to be compressed slightly to ease the North Star into the quilt. The entire background is a pattern of quilted stars.

The present owners purchased this celestial view from a dealer in San Diego in 1981, who stated that it came from a family in that city. While we do not know the quilter's name, we do know that she envisioned this clear, starry night and left us a specific glimpse of her world.

Nosegay

At the age of thirteen or fourteen, Florence Rebecca Howe left school and learned to operate a power sewing machine in a factory to help support her family. She was one of seven children born in Detroit, Michigan, to a cooper and his wife. When she married Mr. Kendburg, a glassblower, she was in her late teens, and a daughter was born to them in 1904. Florence was widowed five years later.

She raised her daughter in Michigan and in the 1920s married James Cronin. During the twenties, she played sheet music in the local music stores of Detroit. She had always played by ear, and it was for this job that she learned to read music. She performed on the accordian and mandolin as well.

Florence also played piano at the early movie houses. The selection of background music was originally left to the discretion of the pianist. Later, specific musical selections were indicated, or scores were prepared to help create the atmosphere and mood for scenes of love, death, or violence. Florence's job was to match the rhythm of the music to the rhythm of the film—supporting it, not competing with it.

There were periods of time when she was not required to play at all, and it was during those breaks that she would quilt, tat, or crochet. Obviously, her hands were never idle.

In the late 1920s, Florence and her husband came to California, where James worked as a wool salesman. With another salesman, James traveled through California, and Florence accompanied them, quilting and acquiring her assorted materials.

Florence loved California, and her enthusiasm helped bring others here, too: her daughter, son-in-law, and grandchild, followed by her mother, three sisters, and a brother.

From 1923 to 1940, Florence played with her all-girl orchestra, The Silver Strings. They practiced every Friday at the home of one or another member (they brought their own sandwiches, after which the hostess served coffee and dessert). They performed "at hospitals, at the Oakland Women's City Club, and at old folks' homes."[77] This ensemble of six never accepted payment; they played for fun.

Florence's vitality seemed inexhaustible. She hooked rugs, knitted, crocheted,

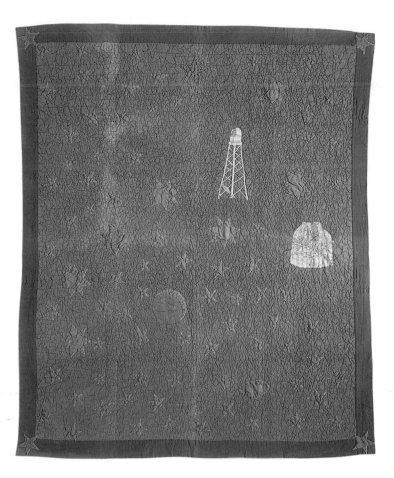

Mount Wilson Observatory Quilt, 1920–1935, made in California. 65″ x 82″. Quiltmaker unknown. Collection of Mary Jane and Sally Van Natta.

Nosegay, 1920–1940, made in Michigan (?). 81″ x 99″. Quiltmaker: Florence Rebecca Howe Kendberg Cronin (1881–1975). Collection of Joyce Beaty.

Dorinda Green Mansfield pictured in front of her home in Woodland, California, with her husband, Edward, and their three sons. 1914–1915.

Dorinda Green Mansfield and her husband, Edward Mansfield, who left Kentucky for California to help their sons avoid lives as sharecroppers.

played her various instruments, and square danced. She continued to drive until she was in her nineties, and crocheted afghans for friends in her last years.

The present owner was given this Nosegay quilt by her grandmother, the quiltmaker, several years before Florence's death. The granddaughter commented, "It is a way of having [grandmother] close to me and it will be passed down through the family so she will always be with us."[78]

Nine-Patch Variation

Dorinda Green was nineteen when she married Edward Mansfield, a tenant farmer in New Orleans, Indiana, in 1889. They lived in Horse Cave, a few miles from Mammoth Cave, Kentucky, in a small house consisting of a kitchen and living room with a loft. There they raised three sons (Dorinda also gave birth to a daughter, who died in infancy). The boys slept in the loft, and during the day their parents' bed was pushed up against the wall of the living room to provide additional space. The quilting frame could then be lowered from the four ceiling hooks on its supporting cords.

One of Dorinda's sons, Alonzo, now ninety-two, remembers women coming to their home for "quiltings." After joining their squares together, they laid down the backing, spread out the cotton, added the top, and attached it all to the four-piece frame. The frame, with its series of holes and pins, allowed them to roll the quilt as the work proceeded. Chalk and string were used to mark the quilting design. "Quiltings" usually occurred when the men got together for some job—hog killing, tobacco planting, or threshing. The quilting and the men's work concluded with a potluck supper.

Dorinda, a seamstress and dressmaker, rode her horse sidesaddle to the homes of various women for whom she sewed. Alonzo recalls that she was a "country seamstress" (meaning that she traveled around) and that she had "all kinds of sewing machines."

Ten years after their marriage, Dorinda and Edward brought their three sons to California in a move prompted by their desire to find better education for the boys so as to help them avoid future lives as sharecroppers. Country schooling in Kentucky was, they felt, too limited and the opportunities too few. They arrived by train in Sacramento on Christmas Eve, 1907. With them was Dorinda's treadle machine, wrapped in quilts.

Before leaving, Edward had placed an order through the Sears catalog for two .38 revolvers. He made holsters, one for himself and one for his oldest son, George. They anticipated a wild jungle! A memorable part of the trip was their seeing, in Kansas, their first Indian, and in Salt Lake City their first Chinese.

Good friends, who had urged them to come to Woodland, found them a house and located jobs for Edward and George. Dorinda, a great cook, worked for wealthy people in the area, baking for their weddings and parties. Later, she became a caterer, famed for her pastries. In Woodland, her quilting was done with the Church Missionary Society rather than at home.

Fabrics in this Nine-Patch quilt were collected over a period of thirty years or more, with some dating to the 1890s. It is quilted in a Fan or wave pattern, probably drawn with the chalk and string that Alonzo describes. Alonzo ("Pops") gave this quilt to a friend, who is the present owner.

Going to Chicago

Gathering fabrics from the family scrap bag, Jettie Starr Camp worked on this quilt for several years, and completed it for her daughter's high school graduation gift in 1932. As there were nine children in the family, the scrap bag was probably well supplied.

Jettie was born in 1879, and at twenty-two married Josiah Washington Camp. He worked variously as farmer, oil-field hand, carpenter, and railway mechanic in

Nine-Patch Variation, 1920–1940, made in California. 68″ x 81″. Quiltmaker: Dorinda Green Mansfield (1870–1953). Collection of Linda Fielding.

Going to Chicago, 1920–1940, made in Texas. 69″ x 79″. Quiltmaker: Jettie Starr Camp (1879–1948). Collection of Mrs. Vera Glendenning.

Jettie Starr Camp, the maker of Going to Chicago, *with one of her nine children.*

Palestine, Texas, where Jettie was born and buried, having spent her entire life there.

Jettie's daughter Vera, who received the quilt, said it was important for "the love and time [her] mother put into this quilt and her ability to put it together with such small pieces...a warm feeling to see how she did it for nine children."[79] We know she made quilts from necessity—to keep her children warm. We also know she could have warmed them with less piecing and fewer colors, so her quilts reflect the satisfaction of other needs as well. She created something beautiful out of what she had, turned the chaos of her scrap bag into an organized, orderly arrangement, and gave her daughter something of great value when she had little.

When Vera took the Greyhound bus from Palestine, Texas, to California in 1942 to find work, she brought the quilt with her. Patches of shirts, skirts, and dresses of her siblings reminded her of home. The quilt still belongs to the daughter of the quiltmaker.

Trip Around the World

During the Great Depression, around 1933–1935, the American Legion Post #55 in Easton, California, held a fund-raising quilt raffle. The current owner of this quilt, a granddaughter of the raffle winner, describes the event:

> My mother was at the hall the night my grandmother won the quilt. Although she was very young at the time, she did remember that the tickets were *very* expensive [perhaps as much as twenty-five cents each] and my grandmother could afford only one ticket....My mother still remembers how exciting it was to win the quilt.[80]

Because of the unusually small size of the pieced squares, this was considered by the family to be a child's quilt. Therefore, it was played with and used. It is hand-pieced and quilted in an overall diagonal pattern.

Information about the quiltmaker was given at the time of the drawing. The owner says, "I was told that the quiltmaker was a migrant worker living in a migrant camp...[and] that she made the quilt to raise money for food for her children."[81]

On the occasion of her daughter's birth in 1976, the present owner received this quilt from her maternal grandmother.

Hollywood Quilt: "Cast of Thousands"

Hollywood cast a magic spell in the 1920s. Among those caught up in its aura was the maker of this unusual quilt. Here are all her favorite stars—121 of them—ranging from Rin Tin Tin, Laurel and Hardy, and Joan Crawford, to Greta Garbo and Mary Pickford. George Bernard Shaw and Lawrence Tibbett also appear among this "cast of thousands."

The drawings, many of which appear to be from cartoons, are embroidered in blue outline stitch on muslin. One block with a cross reads, "The Bowl Cross, Hollywood" and adds, somewhat loftily, "art...music...literature." That particular monument, Hollywood (Bowl) Cross for Pilgrimage, no longer exists.

There is no record of the quiltmaker's name, but we do know she was moved by the glamour of Hollywood celebrities to devote hours to creating their likenesses on this embroidered and unquilted top.

Mary Jane Van Natta and her daughter, Sally, have been collecting quilts for about twenty years. Among the quilts that appeal to them are those which are unique, one-of-a-kind pieces. Mary Jane commented that she was attracted to unusual quilts because of "the simplicity and innocence of their makers in using a quilt to express their emotions or to celebrate something they found more exciting than a pattern would be."[82] This quilt was purchased from an antiques dealer in Santa Barbara just a few years ago.

Trip Around the World, Postage
Stamp Quilt, 1925–1935, made in
California. 61″ x 74″. Quiltmaker
unknown. Collection of Linda
Gilfillan McAlexander.

Hollywood Quilt, 1925–1935, made in California. 73″ x 86″. Quilt-maker unknown. Detail included. Collection of Mary Jane and Sally Van Natta.

Blazing Star Variation, family name: Grandma's Dream, 1932, made in Colorado. 72″ x 79″. Quiltmaker: Pearl Pryor Millsap (1883–1975). Detail included. Collection of Gladys A. Killion.

Blazing Star Variation and Pine Tree

Cordelia Pryor divided her time between the homes of her three daughters, living with each in turn, much as her own mother, a quiltmaker, had spent years in Cordelia's own household. Just outside the Colorado farm home of Pearl Pryor Millsap, Cordelia's eldest daughter, was a cherry orchard where mother and daughter had been picking fruit for canning. That night, sprightly red birds clutching cherries in their beaks appeared in a dream in which Cordelia envisioned the design of an entire quilt. Duly inspired, her daughter Pearl created this quilt according to her mother's description of the dream.

Pearl ("Aunt Perdie") was born in 1883 in Leon, Iowa, the eldest of four children. She was immersed in quilting and needlework of all kinds, especially because a grandmother lived with the family and was an avid quiltmaker. Pearl lived at home until her marriage to Glen Millsap, a farmer, around 1906. In 1909, with other family members, they homesteaded in eastern Colorado, where their homestead house is still standing. Their final papers, signed by Woodrow Wilson, certified their compliance with the Homestead Act. They had built and lived in their home on a barren, windswept plain thirty miles from the nearest railroad, a two-day journey by lumber wagon.

Pearl Pryor Millsap, left, pictured at age twenty-one, with two younger sisters, Ruby, sixteen, and Lucille, ten. 1904.

When more homesteaders arrived, a school was built and Pearl rode horseback the two and one half miles to her teaching post in the rural one-room Red Top school. Riding with Pearl on the horse (with arms clinging around Pearl's waist) was her niece, who would one day inherit and treasure her aunt's work.

It was while living in Colorado that Pearl made both Grandma's Dream and the Pine Tree quilts. An accomplished musician, Pearl also taught piano and painted, and her family still owns several of her works.

In her Pine Tree quilt, Pearl painted directly onto the fabric. Her pine cones "were colored from dye she prepared from prairie grasses."[83] The needles are painted and each one is stuffed, then outline quilted. Pearl learned to quilt from her grandmother, whose quilts she inherited.

In Grandma's Dream, her charming appliquéd vases alternate with quilted feather plumes, stitched in double lines in the open areas. A crosshatch pattern of quilting covers the background, and the center of the star contains a large feather wreath that encircles the appliqué wreath.

In 1937, Pearl and her husband moved to San Diego, where she taught school. When she was eighty, Pearl signed up for classes in San Diego to study Spanish, became proficient, and was written up in a San Diego newspaper article giving special attention to her accomplishments. At ninety, in a nursing home, she served as Spanish interpreter for staff and patients.

The present owner of the quilts is Pearl's niece, who says, "Aunt Perdie was my favorite aunt . . . my mother's older talented sister."[84] Aunt Perdie raised an adopted nephew and had no direct descendants.

Delectable Mountains Variation

A somewhat independent young woman in her early twenties, Irene Garner wanted to leave the small-town atmosphere of her Iowa upbringing to look for work and "to look for opportunity on the West Coast." In 1927, she drove with friends to California, where she became a high school sewing teacher. It was when she returned for a summer visit to the Midwest that she went to Nuark, Illinois, to see her aunt, at whose home a quilt was displayed.

Quiltmaking was not new to the women in the Lutheran church group in Nuark. Their expertise was evident in the beautiful example displayed in the living room at Irene's aunt's home.

Upon seeing the quilt made by her aunt's church group, Irene commented, "Oh, I would love one." Her admiring comment was taken literally, and a couple of years

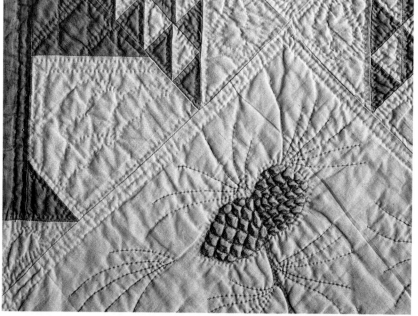

Pine Tree, family name: The Pine Cone Quilt, 1925–1935, made in Colorado. 73″ x 94″. Quiltmaker: Pearl Pryor Millsap (1883–1975). Detail included. Collection of Gladys A. Killion.

Delectable Mountains Variation, family name: The Butterfly Quilt, 1932–1933, made in Illinois. 78″ x 80″. Quiltmaker: the Lutheran Church Quilting Group of Nuark, Illinois. Collection of Irene Nelson Garner and Robin Guzman.

Crazy Quilt, 1925–1940, made in California. 69″ x 88″. Quiltmaker: Mary Margaret Ragatz Alexander (1892–1986). Collection of Wendy Louise Eads.

Starburst, 1930–1935, made in California. 62″ x 76″. Quiltmaker: Ruth Estelle King Wofford Heffington (1887–1970). Collection of Mrs. Martha Wofford Fields.

later, during the depths of the Great Depression, a C.O.D. package arrived for Irene. It had been sent to California from the quilting group in Illinois; in the package was this quilt with butterflies flitting through it in exquisite quilting.

Although she had forgotten her somewhat casual placement of an order, she paid for it, even though "the price of $25 was considerable money in those hard times [1933] and as Aunt Irene says, 'I never really cared for butterflies.' She kept the quilt, acknowledging its craftsmanship and beauty."[85]

The present owner, a great-grandniece of Irene's, says, "It is fortunate for us that Aunt Irene did not find butterflies more appealing. Because of this, she kept this wonderful quilt tucked away."[86]

Crazy Quilt

Mary Margaret Ragatz was born in 1894 in Gettysburg, South Dakota, to Mennonite parents who had immigrated from Switzerland. As Swiss law decreed that only eldest sons could inherit, her father, a younger son, had sought a new life and farmland in America.

It was a strict, God-fearing home in which Mary was raised, and her mother, Salome Nold Ragatz, a midwife, brought over one hundred babies into the rural prairie world where doctors were rarely available.

Mary's father, a member of the local school board, agreed to take his turn at housing the new schoolteacher, Charles Morey Alexander. Family history relates that Charles walked into their home, saw Mary sewing, and was certain that here was the girl he wanted to marry. After their marriage they raised five children and lived a thrifty, simple life. Mary had learned to sew at five or six, and is remembered to have always had needlework in her hands.

Charles left schoolteaching in South Dakota to become a photojournalist, and it was during this career that they moved to California. The Depression hit, and he was out of work until he found eventual employment in the Federal Writers Project.

It was in the late 1920s that Mary started her Crazy quilt, using fabrics that came from South Dakota in her scrap bag. Included were remnants from dressmaking, as well as scraps from her mother's and aunts' blouses and sunbonnets of the late 1800s. The rest came by way of a "windfall" that is described by Mary's granddaughter: "My grandfather had signed up for various programs of government relief. As a result the family, including five children, regularly received packages of clothing, shoes and other articles."[87] Government subsidized workers, who sewed the garments, apparently knew little about sewing, however.

> Most of the clothing was unwearable due to overlarge shoulders and neck openings, and armholes and sleeves too small to fit an arm through...the fabric was brand new, so my grandmother salvaged what she could...and made the rest into crazy quilts.[88]

Charles next became a city clerk, and then determined to join his two brothers, who had "gold fever" and were prospecting in northern California. In 1940, he and Mary moved to an area with creek water and no electricity, a good ten miles from town. Here, Mary set up her quilting frame, gardened, made soap, and lived a simple life in idyllic country near the Oregon border. She often quilted outdoors, propping the frame on crates or furniture. Indoors, the frame rested on chairs near the kitchen stove—the only area of the house kept warm enough for quilting. She made her patterns out of anything—paper, cardboard, or whatever she could find.

Mary made quilts for everyone in the family, including aunts and uncles. This tied Crazy quilt, which she made for herself and her husband on her treadle machine, now belongs to her granddaughter, who has also inherited the machine that was "in constant use by [her] grandmother up until her death...this year at age 94."[89]

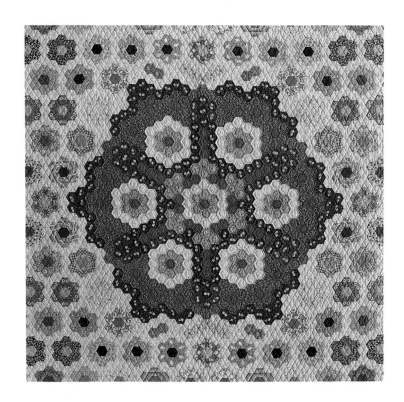

Hexagon Medallion, 1930–1935,
made in California. 79″ x 85″.
Quiltmaker: Myrtle Dunn (b.
1904). Detail included. Collection
of Myrtle Dunn.

Starburst

Born into an Arkansas family near Heber Springs in 1887, Ruth Estelle (Essie) King spent her childhood on the family farm and was married at about age twenty-one to James Dentis ("Dent") Wofford. When thirty-year-old "Dent" died ten years later, Essie was left with four young children to care for.

Benjamin Franklin Heffington, an older man with four nearly grown boys of his own, became Essie's second husband, and they had four more children. Ben was a "drinking man and moved frequently, selling or giving Essie's quilts away."[90] He died of mastitis in the early 1930s, leaving Essie widowed for a second time.

It was probably in the thirties that Essie came to California. She made this tied quilt during the worst of the Great Depression while living in the area of Merced, California, and presented it to her son when he was married in 1935.

A petite but strong woman, Essie managed to hold her large family together during the most difficult times. Always poor, they all worked at fruit picking and farming and wherever they could find jobs.

Tobacco pouches, flour sacks, and old clothes were her customary and readily available sources of material. She hand-dyed these cotton fabrics for use in her quilts. Essie took snuff and chewed tobacco regularly, smoking a pipe "only when it was inconvenient to spit," so she was her own source of tobacco pouches. She also prevailed upon her sons to save these tokens of their smoking habits.

Of the many quilts Essie made, this is the only one known to remain. It now belongs to her granddaughter, a graphic and striking reminder of this plucky quiltmaker.

Ruth Estelle King Wofford Heffington, maker of the Starburst, at home. 1957.

Hexagon Medallion

A Stockton couple drove their pickup truck to a San Francisco factory that made dresses and aprons and loaded the truck with leftover cut-fabric pieces. A hobby was thus transformed into a small business in the heart of the Depression.

The dress factory offered all the fabric free, provided the recipients agreed to carry off an entire ton. Several trips were required to haul all the material back to the apartment, where much of it was stored in the basement. The quiltmaker was delighted with the colors and patterns that seemed perfect for her quilts.

Just ten years earlier, in 1923, Myrtle Grace Hibbard had married builder Phil S. Dunn in Los Angeles. After several years there, they moved to Stockton, about the time the Depression devastated the construction business. There was no construction work—indeed, no work of any kind. The Dunns managed an apartment house of eight units and searched for other sources of income.

Myrtle had made several quilts and considered quiltmaking to be a hobby. Many friends who admired her work asked for patterns and help, and their interest, coupled with a magazine article about making money at home, sparked her decision to make up quilt kits.

Working together, the Dunns cut cardboard patterns and offered the quilt kits in two ways: customers could buy patterns along with the fabric, or they could get the pieces precut. To cut the material, Myrtle used her cardboard templates and her scissors, cutting by hand through three or four layers of fabric at a time.

Myrtle found the Depression a time when "[everyone] helped one another." She traded her kits for vegetables, chickens, eggs, fruits, or nuts—whatever anyone had to barter. Occasionally she received cash, but she especially wanted to make her kits accessible to everyone. Her patterns included Log Cabins, Wedding Rings, Stars, and appliqué designs. Along with the kit, a buyer received the reassurance that if problems arose, she could return for help! Myrtle's two small children spent many hours playing under her quilting frame.

After delivering her Hexagon Medallion to Sacramento for entry in the

Myrtle Dunn, whose quilt hobby became a kit business and provided income during the Depression, is pictured here around 1928 with her husband, Phil S. Dunn, who assisted her on this project.

World's Fair Map Quilt, 1933,
made in Idaho. 87″ x 71″. Quiltmaker: Myrtle Louise Black Collord (1890–1980). Collection of
James and Marjorie Collord.

California State Fair in the early 1930s, Myrtle was unable to attend the fair. She recalls that they did not have the money for the attendance fee. It wasn't until she picked up her quilt and found a blue ribbon attached that she knew it had received an award, sharing first prize with another quiltmaker, Louise Lyons of Turlock.

Myrtle's quilt kits saw her family through some difficult years and brought many rewards. Recollections of the Depression also include times of joy and warmth because people "stuck together."

This last remaining example of her kit business is still in Myrtle's possession. She says, "My children want this quilt kept in the family as a sample of the work I did during those Depression years."

World's Fair Map Quilt

In 1933 the Chicago Century of Progress Exposition attracted the attention of quilters all over the country, and 24,878 quilts were delivered to local Sears stores or to Sears mail-order houses for inclusion in this special competition. Local winners were forwarded to regional competitions, and final selections were exhibited in the Sears building at the Century of Progress fair.

Among the entrants was Myrtle Louise Black Collord, whose quilt was entered from Idaho. Born in Orderville, Utah, she had moved to Tetonia, Idaho, where she went to school and married Roscoe Collord. After she and Roscoe moved to Rupert, Myrtle learned quilting from her neighbors and from a church group. Myrtle had one son and one adopted daughter.

The Collord's move to California included roadside camping in a tent. Pictured is Myrtle's sister-in-law, Savanah Collord. 1934–1935.

Her quilt, depicting a map of the world bordered by flags of all nations, won a ribbon. The map had been colored by her seventeen-year-old son, James, using crayon on cotton material; he also drew to scale the countries for her appliquéd map. James states that she was "the best seamstress in the state of Idaho, and she made shirts for husband, son, and [her] six brothers."[91]

A spare bedroom was set aside for Myrtle's quilting. Although she often worked alone, when she met with others, their quilting together provided Myrtle her primary social activity.

James, who had left home to look for work, said that when he saw his mother four months after she had received her notification letter and ribbon in the mail, she was "still pretty excited."

The Great Depression sent many families off to California in a determined and sometimes desperate search for a better life. One family describes having two flats every day of the entire trip. The Collords, with their daughter of six or seven, left Idaho driving a Chevy. They cooked out on the trip and searched for inexpensive camps or just stopped along the road. Packed with their belongings was Louise's ribbon-winning quilt.

Roscoe found work in Wilmar, California, near downtown Los Angeles, as an elevator operator with a dry-goods company. His work in the warehouse gave him ample time to remove nails from the sturdy shipping crates. He carried the wood home with him at night, on the streetcar, and used it in building their house.

The quilt has now been inherited by Myrtle's son, who as a boy had colored it.

Myrtle Louise Black Collord proudly shows her World Map Quilt after its return from the 1933 Century of Progress Exposition in Chicago. An award ribbon is attached below the title. With Myrtle is her daughter. 1934.

Cowboy Quilt

An enthusiastic lover of horses, Thelma Norman Ryan decided to make herself a horse quilt. Her drawings were taken from the covers of Westerns, or what were referred to as "dime cowboy novels" (although by 1934, they cost fifteen cents). She then made her drawings into patterns for the intricate appliqués. Her first cowboy quilt was made in cottons, but Thelma wanted something more visible and colorful, so she made this second one of silk. Hand-painting and embroidery add detail.

Born and raised in San Francisco, where her parents ran a hotel, she attended a

125

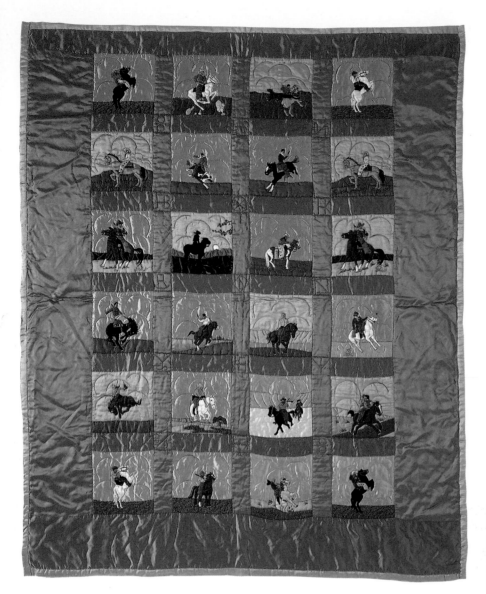

Cowboy Quilt, 1933, made in
California. 71″ x 88″. Quiltmaker:
Thelma Norman Ryan (1908–
1987). Detail included. Collection
of Josie Mattingly.

finishing school there and, upon her marriage to Charles Ryan, a forest-fire lookout, moved to Merimac, California. From there, Thelma accompanied her husband to the various lookouts where he was stationed and lived a decidedly isolated life. She had no children.

The blocks for this quilt were finished in 1933, when Thelma was twenty-five, but it was not quilted until twenty years later. Cattle brands are delineated with quilting stitches where sashings intersect. Thelma's husband was at first somewhat jealous of the attention she received for her work, and he did not encourage her. Later, however, he used quilt patterns as designs in making his inlaid wooden boxes and plates.

A family friend recalls how Thelma directed her artistic ability into her cooking as well. She once presented them with some apricot and apple pies, each of which was decorated with a small pie-crust picture, or appliqué, of the fruit. It was realistically colored and painted, with the whole then glazed to a sheen. The friend still regrets that forks ever pierced those crusts, and she maintains that the exquisitely decorated pies "should never have been eaten."

In 1986, just a year before she died, Thelma gave this Cowboy quilt to her friend Josie Mattingly, who says, "She said I could take better care of it than she. She also said I was the *only* one ever to express interest in the quilt!...She made a corrugated box and painted it green to store the quilt in."

Thelma Norman Ryan, whose love of horses prompted her to make the Cowboy quilt, which was inspired by her collection of cowboy pictures from Western magazines. 1933.

Rebus Puzzle/San Francisco Examiner

A flea market in San Juan Bautista yielded this thirty-five-dollar treasure for its new owner. In 1933, during the depths of the Depression, the *San Francisco Examiner* published a Movie Star Contest with rebus puzzles. Mrs. C. S. Jackson from Lodi transposed those drawings into her quilt. It is pieced, with ink drawings and some hand-coloring on the blocks. Embroidered stitches mimic the broken "cut-here" lines from the newspaper. While retaining an overall structure of traditional quilts, and a familiar block where sashings cross, it is a unique quilt.

By identifying the newspaper and the contest name, as well as including her own signature and the date, Mrs. Jackson has left a significant amount of information about her singular quilt. She also relates, visually, the Californian's early preoccupation with the Hollywood movie industry. Although she finished her quilt top in 1933, it was not quilted until years later by the present owner and friends.

Sunshine and Shadows

The California health boom had its beginnings during the gold rush, when prospectors wrote home about the climate. John Bidwell, who led the first wagon train to California in 1841, wrote back to the Midwest: "Those of the company who came here for their health, were all successful."[92] The popularity of California for the ill, especially for consumptives, peaked in the late 1870s and 1880s, and in 1887–1888 the Great Blizzard in the East sent more people than ever before seeking the milder West Coast climate.

It was the search for a drier environment that prompted Fred and Grace Albro Voorhees to leave Coldwater, Michigan. Born in Lapeer in 1877, Grace was married at twenty-two, and it was her husband Fred's failing health that took them to California.

After their arrival in Montebello, Fred became a streetcar motorman for the Los Angeles Railway Company and a pumper for Union Oil. It was while living in Montebello that Grace made this quilt for her only son, born in 1900. She often quilted while the rest of her family slept, or when her husband worked at night. Remembered by her family as "charming, outgoing, and never idle," she never quite "settled down" to homemaking, although she liked ironing and was known

The San Francisco Examiner *announcement of its Movie Stars Name Contest (a "game of skill") that offered cash prizes. A picture-puzzle was printed with each edition of the paper and clues were broadcast three times a day. 1933.*

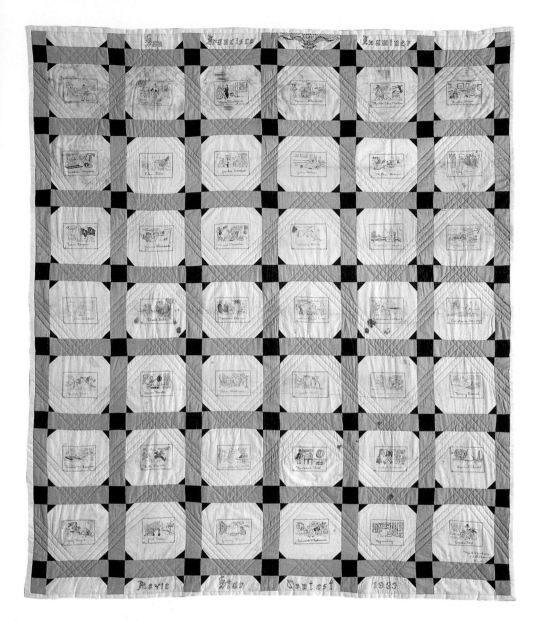

San Francisco Examiner Movie Star Contest Quilt, 1933 (quilted later), made in California. 66″ x 78″. Quiltmaker: C. S. Jackson. Details included. Collection of Marilee Kline.

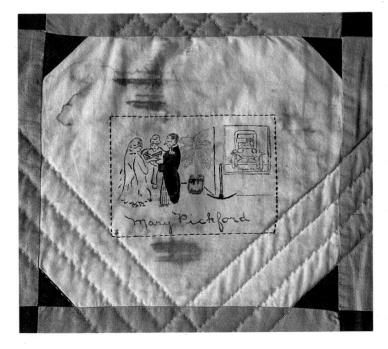

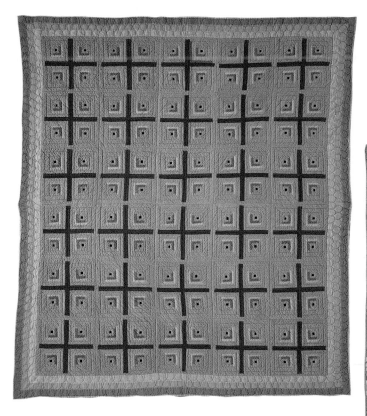

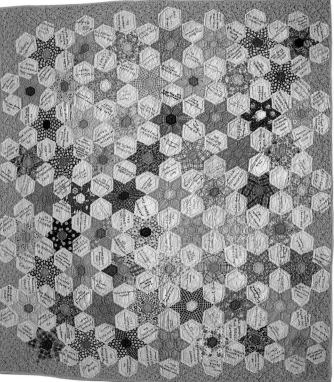

Bias Tape Quilt, Sunshine and Shadows, family name: Log Cabin, 1930–1940, made in California. 73″ x 81″. Quiltmaker: Grace Albra Voorhees (1877-1954). Collection of Jack Baldwin.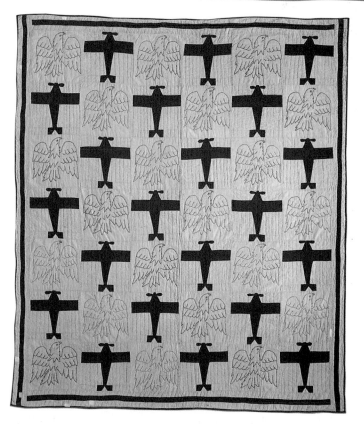

Hexagon Star, 1930–1940, made in California. 74″ x 82″. Quiltmaker: Frances Haley Yancey Barnes (1859-1948). Collection of Joan Kohler Littlefield.

Lone Eagle Quilt, family name: Lindy's Plane, 1930–1940, made in California. 71″ x 85″. Quiltmakers: Mary Morrison Ellis (1860-1940) and Ethel Ellis Nobel (1887-1974). Collection of Mary M. Noble Moore.

Grace Albra Voorhees, on the right, made the Bias Tape Log Cabin, later given to her granddaughter, Vivian, shown holding her doll. The other woman is unidentified.

for her cooking and baking. Always physically active, Grace grew up preferring fishing to being indoors, and chose to exercise her uncle's racehorses rather than pursue domestic chores. Dancing (a favorite pastime well into her sixties), card-playing, and entertaining on a large scale did not eliminate time for crocheting, quilting, and rugmaking. She was the first of her friends to wear lipstick, rouge, and nail polish, and was the first to get a permanent wave. Despite what her family described as her "radical behavior and ideas" and her recounting of mystical experiences, she was a lifelong churchgoer and was active in both the Women's Club and the Eastern Star.

Made from "store-bought" bias tapes in the favorite 1930s colors of apple green and orchid, Grace's quilt is devised in such a way as to take advantage of a relatively new product and incorporate it into the work. It was hand-quilted later by the women in her church with in-the-ditch stitches on the top and teacup quilting on the border. Grace's name and the dates of her birth and death were embroidered in outline stitches.

Grace's great-grandson is the present owner of this unusual quilt.

Hexagon Star (Friendship)

In 1884, at the age of twenty-five, Frances Haley Yancey married Andrew Jackson Barnes. When they left Woodstock, Georgia, Frances said good-bye to her grandfather, who farmed, her grandmother, and her mother, who taught school. Her father had died when she was five. She also left acquaintances from the Cherokee Mills rope factory, where she had worked as a child to supplement the family income.

After living in Texas for six years, Frances and her husband, a farmer and grocer, came to California in search of better land and greater opportunities. Three of their five children had already been born when they made the trip by train and settled in Modesto, California.

In 1930, at the age of seventy-one, Frances started a quilted remembrance of friends and relatives from Georgia, Texas, Alabama, Florida, and California. She sent fabric to each person on which they were to write their names. Some were returned already embroidered; others were stitched in multicolors by Frances and her two daughters-in-law, Ida Bailey Barnes and Ethel Thorne Barnes.

The hexagons contain nearly one hundred names, many with addresses and/or occupations. Frances made a block for Lloyd Barnes, her oldest grandchild, who had drowned in 1912 at the age of thirteen; another block commemorated Father Yancey, who died in the Civil War. A block for herself was inscribed Tad Yancey, Toonigh, Georgia. ("Tadpole" had been her childhood nickname.) Other blocks included these inscriptions:

> *Alfred Janzen, Delivery Man, Modesto, Ca.*
> *Doctor Maltby, Hickory Flat, Ga.*
> *Frank O'Brien, Laundry Man, Modesto, Ca.*

Everyone who had been a part of her life was included, and among them were the doctor who delivered Frances's daughter Mary in 1894, several ministers, attorneys, a motor cop, relatives, and Mrs. Bryce, the landlady of the boarding-house where daughter Mary's husband had resided before his marriage.

Frances had learned quilting from her mother, who started her sewing at age five, and this is one of the many quilts that she made. Years later, she quilted with a church group at Methodist Episcopal South. This Signature quilt passed from Frances to her daughter-in-law Ida, then to Ida's daughter Iris. Iris passed it along to her cousin, a granddaughter of the maker, when she discovered the cousin's last name (Littlefield) in the quilt. Although the quilt is hand-pieced, its binding is

Francis Haley Yancey Barnes seen in the back yard of her home in Modesto, California. With her are her grandchildren, Ordeene Reinitz, Jary Barnes, Ann Barnes, Dick Beinitz, and Joan Kohler (the present owner of the quilt).

added with machine stitching. Hand-quilted lines parallel the seams of hexagons and stars, whereas the green print edges are crosshatched.

Lone Eagle Quilt

Charles Lindbergh's nonstop flight across the Atlantic in 1927 electrified the world and made him a hero to millions of people whose imaginations he fired. He inspired adventure, influenced politics, attracted an alarming amount of attention, and was even honored with quilts designed to commemorate his famous flight. The January 1929 *Successful Farming* magazine advertised and pictured a Lone Eagle quilt, giving a description of the development of its design. The designer, Emma S. Tyrell, said:

> Having watched planes fly over our city and having seen pictures of them, I was quite sure I knew all about their design. So I started to draw my patterns with all the confidence of an expert. But before it was finished I found that my observance had not been so keen. There was more than one little detail puzzling me. My first assistance came to me from the toy plane designed from the Spirit of St. Louis.
>
> Finally I consulted a friend of mine who is a pilot. He was most interested in helping me with correct proportions and all of the finer points.[93]

Mary Morrison Ellis, seated on the right, is pictured with her family. In the back row is her son, Roy; her son-in-law, Bert Noble; daughter, Ethel Ellis Noble; and daughter, Nelia. In front are her husband, James Ellis, and Ethel's daughter, Mary Noble. Mary and Ethel worked jointly on the Lindy's Plane quilt, and were often joined in their quilting by Nelia.

Emma Tyrell's original piece in yellow and white broadcloth was designed to be either pieced or appliquéd, and directions were offered. At the close of the article, a pamphlet called "Old-time Quilting" was offered for sale for ten cents.

Among the many women who were inspired to re-create these designs from magazines were a mother-daughter quilting team—Mary Morrison Ellis and Ethel Ellis Noble. Mary, born in Kentucky, and her daughter Ethel, born in Missouri, made many quilts together. Both were married to farmers, and they eventually all moved to California, traveling west in a Model T.

Among the quilts they made jointly was this pieced airplane made for Ethel's sons' room, after their move to Lindsay, California. The older boy was seventeen or eighteen and his brother was just five or six, but both were fascinated by airplanes. (The quilt was not to be used on the bed until the little one had stopped wetting it!)

Ethel's husband, who ran the Noble Grocery Store in Lindsay, built her a quilt frame that was kept on their big back porch. At the end of the day, one edge of the quilt was pulled up to the ceiling on cords, so the frame could be leaned against the wall and the porch converted to another bedroom.

Ethel and her mother (who lived with her), along with a sister-in-law from next door, made many quilts, ordering their patterns through magazines. Ethel's mother, Mary, noted in her journal that they paid ten cents a yard for material at the local mercantile.

Their Lindy's Airplane quilt alternates pieced planes with blocks in which the eagles have been drawn and stitched onto the fabric. The quilt, which now belongs to Ethel's daughter, has a quilting pattern of lines running vertically through the airplane blocks.

Flour Bag Quilt

The need to "make do" was keenly felt during the Depression, and the satisfactions that came from making do with flour sacks were several. Not only were the bags and labels colorful, but they housed the essential "staff of life." Furthermore, they

Flour Bag Quilt (Ice Cream Cone Border), 1930–1940, made in Nebraska (?). 68″ x 81″. Quiltmaker unknown. Detail included. Collection of Betty Head.

were seen as a bonus since they were usually free. The use of these bags was an extension of other similar salvaging efforts. Years before, cigar ribbons had been collected, just as cotton tobacco pouches were later retrieved when smokers discarded them. Satin ties from funeral bouquets were salvaged from cemeteries. Sugar and rice bags were also a ready source of decorative and inexpensive material.

The all-cotton, plain-weave flour bags were usually printed in an all-over pattern, appropriate for clothing, although the prints were often deliberately eradicated by bleaching to prepare the material for use in undergarments or utilitarian quilts. Few quilts made from flour sacks actually *feature* the labels as this one does, although the Belgian women, thanking Herbert Hoover for the Food Relief program during World War I, sent him beautifully embroidered panels, many worked on flour and sugar sacks. These emblems, trademarks, and words had wonderfully familiar appeal as medallion-type designs.

To retain the color, the trademarked fabrics were sometimes treated with vinegar in an attempt to "set" the dyes. The bright colors of the bags in this quilt suggest that they were printed in the 1930s when, for the first time, a wide range of colors was used in their printing. Gathering or collecting pretty examples of sack designs became a fad, or a friendly competition, about that time. There was often a theme to a collection: one might gather all flowers, or find designs from various cities or mills. Sometimes the rivalry centered on acquiring a sack from the most distant location, with women exchanging bags to gain variety.[94]

Bagging companies promoted the use of cotton bags long after paper bags might have proven less expensive. In their promotions they urged commercial bakers to consider that they could resell their cotton bags.

This colorfully embroidered quilt made from flour bags was spotted by a woman, newly interested in quilts, who was attending the Shasta County coroner's auction in 1976. She noticed, in a large box of bedding, a bit of the colorful embroidery showing. Insisting that her husband bid on the box, she watched as his ten-dollar bid successfully bought the quilt.

The name of a town is included on each block—perhaps the town in which the mill was located, information that may have appeared on another part of the bag. These include Beatrice, Hastings, Lexington, and Crete, Nebraska, along with Blue Rapids, Kansas. No name, date, or hometown appears to offer clues about the quiltmaker. She probably lived in Kansas or Nebraska, where she embroidered, with infinite patience, all the colored areas with embroidery floss. The Fan or Ice Cream Cone border is unpadded and unquilted, whereas the blocks are quilted in hanging diamonds with cables over the sashing.

Hexagon Star

In 1892, sixteen-year-old Susan Ingram married John Luis Meadows in Arkansas, where both had been raised. John's mother, Lucinda, who was of Cherokee descent, had married John Meadows (Meaders), a farmer, and they lived in a dug-out house.

Susan and John came west in 1905 with their three daughters; they joined Susan's parents, who had come two years earlier, and John's parents. Susan's daughters recall that the train ride lasted several days and that all the windows were kept closed. As there were no berths on the train, they bundled up in blankets and spent the nights curled up in their seats to sleep. The train made scheduled stops at stations where passengers could disembark and have a meal while the train waited.

Two of Susan's three daughters remember summers spent quilting with their grandmother Lucinda Meadows. Since "everybody made their own clothes,"[95] Lucinda exchanged scraps with friends and cut her patterns from cardboard. When sunlight was at its best, the girls quilted at the easily reached edges of the frame, while their grandmother quilted the middle. When sunlight faded, they rolled the quilted section to prepare it for the following day's work. The frame, suspended from the ceiling by the cords tied at the four corners, was hoisted ceilingward until the next day.

Both of the girls remained childless. Susan's grandson says, "They swear to this day their summers living with their Indian grandmother resulted in a childless life due to herbaceous remedies. Needless to say, my own grandmother, the oldest (of the three girls) didn't go (to visit)."[96]

The Meadows' move west started with John's work building railway depots and ended in the Imperial Valley, where they purchased land and started a dairy that grew to include 150 cows. They built their own house and sheds, and Susan's life was one of hard physical work, cooking with a wood fire, washing clothes in tubs, and preparing chicken dinners "from scratch" (which meant wringing the chickens' necks). It was during these years that she started quilting.

Susan's grandson recalled that she made "the world's best divinity candy," which he "traded for rides on Harry Brown's bicycle."[97] Apparently, she produced an ample supply, for he was able to barter for enough rides to give himself a case of heat stroke.

The Meadows eventually sold their dairy and bought a motel. When John died in 1932, Susan moved to a small house in Long Beach and continued to make quilts.

Susan's grandson owns this Hexagon Star, probably made after the move to Long Beach, when she relied less on scraps and more on purchased material. He comments: "It represents a genuine link between generations and a tangible piece of our great-grandmother's mind and soul. Because of this quilt, she is our most unforgettable ancestor."[98]

Double Wedding Ring with Brands

Little is known about the maker of this quilt other than that she was born in 1885 in Ventura County and eventually became Mrs. Burke.

After the quilt was pieced, assembled, and quilted, the twenty-seven different cattle brands were added with black embroidery in the open areas. One of the brands, "ERN," is from the Ernie Righetti Nuney ranch, after which the Righetti High School in Santa Monica is named.

The machine-quilting in the border of this work utilizes a freestyle approach; the centers of its blocks are quite unrestrained by traditional patterns, varying from block to block. The addition of the brand designs tells us only that they had some significance in the quilter's life. Her strongly contrasting solid colors in an unusual combination with delicately patterned materials offer a glimpse of a woman who was not restricted by the conventions of her craft. The quilt was found in a Ventura antiques shop in 1975.

Grandmother's Flower Garden

When Snow White sang "Someday My Prince Will Come" in the first full-length animated cartoon feature in 1938, Walt Disney created an instant heroine for America. Mickey Mouse, introduced just ten years earlier, and the ubiquitous Donald Duck and Pluto, had already permeated advertising and promotion worldwide.

Like other Disney creations, Snow White appeared on fabric, to the delight of consumers. Mae Jensen collected fabrics from her grandchildren's clothes for a quilt, and among the fabrics was a pair of pajamas featuring Snow White. Mae cut the figures out and carefully placed one in the center of each circle of hexagons, thus combining "making do" with the "latest thing," as Grandmother brings Snow White into her flower garden.

Mae Berthea Roberts was born in 1869 in Greenwood, Minnesota. Her ancestors had moved to South Dakota and Minnesota before the areas became states, and she

Hexagon Star, 1930–1940, made in California. 72″ x 81″. Quiltmaker: Susan Ingram Meadows (Meaders) (1892–1956). Collection of Donna and Vincent Bezdecheck.

Double Wedding Ring with Brands, 1930–1940, made in California. 68″ x 83″. Quiltmaker: Mrs. Burke. Collection of Mary Jane and Sally Van Natta.

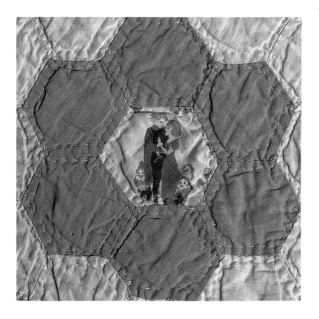

Grandmother's Flower Garden, family name: Gram's Quilt, 1930–1940, made in California. 74″ x 79″. Quiltmaker: Mae Bethea Roberts Ruhberg Jensen (1869–1967). Detail included. Collection of Emily Ruhberg Louw.

was keenly interested and very involved in the history of that area. Mae had been the first woman enrolled in North Dakota University when it was founded, according to her family.

She married George Ruhlberg, a salesman, in 1891 and was a homemaker and landlady. She raised one son, who became a psychiatrist and neurologist. After she was widowed in the early 1920s, she headed for California, where she met Jack Jensen; they were married when she was fifty-six.

Family recollections place the making of the quilt in 1939, although many of the fabrics date to much earlier. On Christmas Day 1940, it was presented to her son's family of five children.

Mae died at age ninety-eight in Santa Barbara. The present owner of the quilt is Mae's granddaughter.

Original Dresden Plate

A plantation in Brunswich-Sheraton, Missouri, was the birthplace of Katura Elisabeth Davis. In 1873, at age twenty-one, she married Lon Tooley, a banker, and embarked on her long career of homemaking and motherhood.

Katura (Kate) attended Stephens College in Columbia, Missouri, for a two-year course when she was seventeen and eighteen. Years later, in the *Alumnae News*, she recalled courses in art, music, and elocution. She said:

> The sole purpose of those early boarding schools was to give a cultural background to the daughters of wealthier planters in the small towns and communities. When we returned home, our college education, pitifully meager though it was, gave us a definite prestige in our community.[99]

Katura Elisabeth Davis Tooley, who drafted and appliquéd her original Dresden Plate quilt. 1910.

Kate gave birth to five children, two of whom died in infancy. In 1902, when a bookkeeper reportedly expanded his own funds at the expense of her husband's bank, they moved to Indian Territory in Oklahoma and started a new bank.

Always articulate and a "born leader," Kate organized the Methodists ("Everyone in town was a Methodist!") and got a church built. Her success was greatly appreciated; she was urged to become mayor but felt too involved in raising her family.

The Tooleys moved to San Francisco in 1921, and it was then that Kate took up quilting. She was over seventy, but made up for her late start by making over ten quilts in about as many years. Her husband made her a frame, which they set up in the social hall, a large room on the garage level of the house.

Her Dresden Plate, which the family recalls she drafted from the plate herself, was started in the early 1930s and finished in 1935. It is beautifully executed in blind-stitch appliqué, and is signed and dated with elegant medallion designs of letters and numbers. The quilting was "hired"—a group of women came to the house to do the work.

Kate's granddaughter recalls that her grandmother was never without her locket and that she would discuss it with no one. Her husband's photo was on the outside, and it is believed to have contained a lock of hair and a photograph of one of the children she lost.

A granddaughter owns several of Kate's quilts, including her Dresden Plate, about which she recalls, "When Grandmother made this...she said it was for me."

Tulips

Emma Silvius was born to Pennsylvania Dutch parents in Bath, Pennsylvania, in the year 1878. She attended grade school, learned quilting from her mother, and at age twenty-five married Ulysses A. Schall. In 1912, on a visit to California, Ulysses, a farmer, was so intrigued with the valley flatlands (no hills to plow!) that the couple

Original Dresden Plate, 1935, made in California. 80″ x 80″. Quiltmaker: Katura Elisabeth Davis Tooley (1852–1938). Detail included. Collection of Barbara Linse.

One of a set of Dresden plates from which Katura Tooley took the pattern for her quilt.

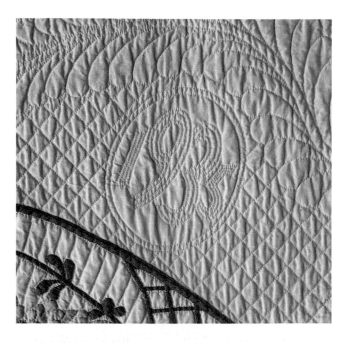

Tulips, family name: Tulip Basket, 1936, made in California. 85″ x 90″. Quiltmaker: Emma Silvius Schall (1878–1969). Collection of W. Royce Oswald.

Ham and Eggs Quilt, Fund Raiser, 1939, made in California. 72″ x 100″. Quiltmakers: Eva Truxillo and Irene Brewster. Detail included. Collection of Mary Jane and Sally Van Natta.

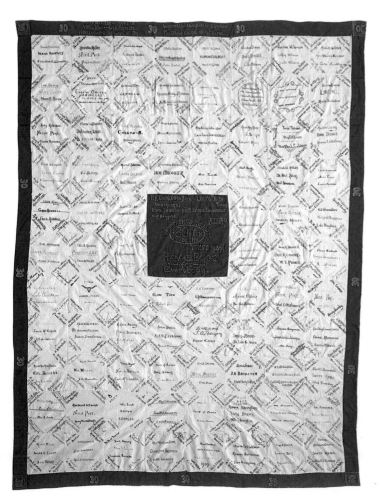

decided to move. It was twelve years later when they came to California to make it their permanent home. Having no children of their own, they brought with them an orphaned child whom they had taken into their home as a daughter in 1919, when the girl was seven.

Instead of buying a ranch in California, which had been the original intention, Ulysses became a technical assistant in Stanford University's Department of Mining and Metallurgy.

Emma's many quilts include the Tulips, which was made as a high school graduation and birthday gift for Walter Royce Oswald. Walter was one of a family of four orphaned children placed in an orphanage in Gilroy, California. He lived with the Schalls in the late 1920s or early 1930s. The year 1936 is commemorated on the quilt in outline stitch. Emma's remaining quilts have gone to friends, and to Dorothy Schall Davies, her daughter, who recalls that Emma had what was referred to as "the quilting room." A quilting frame was set up there, with the four corners resting on four posts. When guests arrived, the frame was lifted off and leaned against the wall, the posts were removed, and the room assumed its more conventional function. Dorothy and Emma often quilted there together. Each year Emma made a quilt as a fund-raiser for the Rebecca's Lodge, an auxiliary group to the I.O.O.F. (International Order of Odd Fellows).

This quilt still belongs to the man for whom it was made. Emma hand-appliquéd her tulips, outlined them with quilting, and stitched additional diagonal lines on each block. In the sashing, she hand-quilted a chain pattern and added a narrow, straight binding to finish this special graduation and birthday present.

Ham and Eggs Quilt

From 1920 to 1930, the over-sixty-five population of Los Angeles and Long Beach increased more than one hundred percent. These new residents, in moving to California, had severed family ties in home areas, an abrupt transition at an age when readjustment is not easy. Many arrived as retirees, looking for easy living, and brought incomes with them. But the collapse of both the stock market and the real estate boom, coupled with the Depression and bank failures, left them needy and sometimes destitute.

In response to this, Upton Sinclair ran for governor in 1934 on a platform promising "To End Poverty in California." The EPIC campaign's advocacy of a monthly pension of fifty dollars for the aged, the handicapped, and widows focused on the many victims of the Depression.

Another development was the Townsend Movement that in 1934–1935 organized older citizens nationwide around the slogan: "Youth for work and age for leisure," along with the promise of a monthly pension of two hundred dollars for every person over sixty, provided that each payment was spent within one month. The passage of the Social Security Act in 1935 did not spell the end of the Townsend Movement.

Variations on the plan were put foward leading to a growing national membership that peaked in 1939 following the recession of 1937–1938 with consequent widespread frustration with the Social Security Act.

The effectiveness of the Townsend organization led to other highly visionary movements—the "Ham and Eggs" program among them. It was proposed as a substitute plan to provide every unemployed person over fifty with a monthly pension of thirty dollars, thus assuring that everyone could afford to eat ham and eggs.

This "Ham and Eggs" quilt is replete with the movement's slogan: "Me and Mine, 100%," "Ham and Eggs for Everybody," and "As California Goes, so Goes Colorado."

Over 850 colorfully embroidered names of individuals, stores, and merchants are included on this machine-pieced and tied quilt. The officers' names are emblazoned in gold satin and outline stitches on a block containing a key slogan: "Retirement Warrants...$30 a week for life." This is undoubtedly the explanation of the "30" that is repeated throughout the border. Eva Truxillo and Irene Brewster, who designed, assembled, and finished the project, also incorporated their own names into the central block.

Presumably, each participant or business contributed money for the privilege of being identified on the quilt, which may also have been raffled or auctioned to raise more funds for the "Ham and Eggs" movement. The Fire Company, Ethelene Bell Rest Home, Uncle Harry's Shop, Lorene and Betty's, and the Ham and Eggs Shop are among the many businesses listed.

The present owners purchased this quilt in 1981. They prefer, they say, the "something different, one-of-a-kind quilt." This is unquestionably the only one of its kind.

Presentation Quilt

A Friendship quilt, bearing the signatures of 274 people from California to Maryland, was presented to Helen G. MacIntosh in 1940. Helen was the Worthy Matron (presiding officer) of the Acantha Chapter #249, Order of the Eastern Star, and the quilt was an expression of appreciation for her work in providing this forum for friendships and shared activities.

The idea for this quilt was that of Worthy Patron, Dr. George A. Boehmer. Inspired by a carpet he had seen, he drew out the design, made the patterns, and cut the templates. His office nurse mailed the fabric pieces to members of the chapter, and to presiding officers of the governing body, the Grand Chapter of California, O.E.S., and they were asked to sign and embroider their names. If they were unable to do the embroidery Mrs. Anita Lane took over the task. Most members lived in the Richmond area.

For one hour each morning, Mrs. Janet M. Hitchcock, sister-in-law of Helen, assembled the blocks. Helen says, "I am sorry that I do not know the name of the Berkeley, California, woman who did the quilting. I do know that this was an avocation and that she did the quilting for fifty dollars."[100]

In addition to established patterns of quilting, the designer added quilted symbols pertinent to the biblical heroines represented by the officers: Ada, symbolized by blue, with sword and veil; Esther, by white, with crown and scepter. Other quilted designs include the shaft of wheat, the broken column, and the cup. The members' signatures, the chapters' name and number, the city, the date, and the names of the honorees are given.

The owner of the quilt wrote in 1988, "A few days ago I celebrated my ninety-first birthday, and among my many happy memories is the presentation of the quilt and the joy I have had using it."[101]

Presentation Quilt

The meeting of the boys' Auto Mechanics Club at the school cafeteria in Tulare Union High School in 1941 concluded with a special dinner and a surprise for Mr. F. Clark Suiter, their teacher and a sponsor of the club. Susie Marie Bellah Monroe, representing the mothers of the boys, presented this quilt to Mr. Suiter.

Born in Lindsay, California, in 1897, Susie graduated from Strathmore High School and married a farmer in the community. Her son, John Monroe, was president (Pilot) of the club in 1940, and Susie is credited with making the quilt. Full of energy and ideas, she was always quick to organize a dinner to acknowledge and honor anyone's contribution to the community. She often quilted with friends and neighbors, but of her many quilts, only this one, with a blanket for filler and quilted in-the-ditch, has survived.

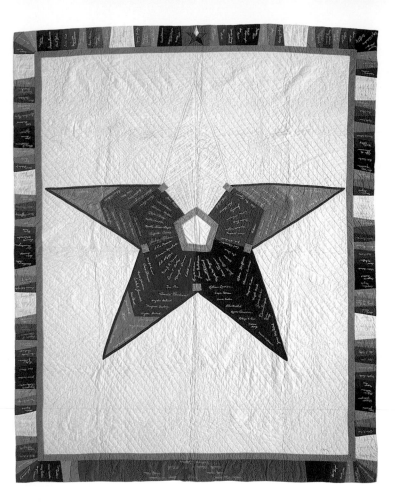

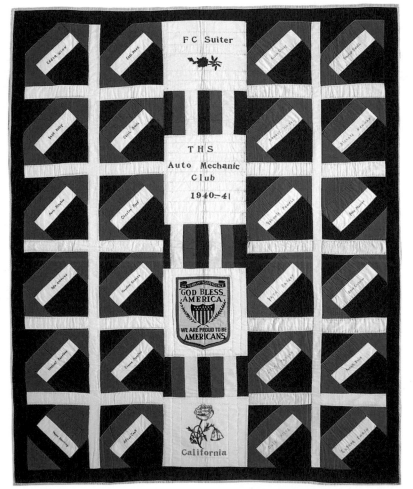

Presentation Quilt, family name: Eastern Star Quilt, 1940, made in California. 79″ x 100″. Quiltmaker: group quilt. Collection of Mrs. Helen G. MacIntosh.

Presentation Quilt, family name: Signature Club Quilt, 1940–1941, made in California. 63″ x 78″. Quiltmaker: Susie Marie Bellah Monroe (1897–1974). Collection of Roberta Suiter Chapin.

When he died in 1947, at age fifty-four, Mr. Suiter was still teaching, as he had for twenty-five years; he had been adviser to the club since 1923. Roberta Suiter Chapin, the present owner of this quilt and the daughter of this honored and influential teacher, has researched the boys' club and the signatures in the quilt, and has traced all but one of the identified club members.

The quilt continues to be treasured for the deep personal affection it represents, but it is also important for its relation to the life and history of a special small town in the San Joaquin Valley. The owner says:

> The names on the quilt reflect the very diverse and rich cultural heritage of the area. Some of the "boys" were living on land that their grandfathers had settled and farmed. Others were the first generation of their families to be born in the United States. The emigration of people out of the Dust Bowl states had occurred only a few years before the quilt was made and some names were of these families who were slowly finding a new place in the community. December 7, 1941, changed all our lives, and particularly this group of men who were interested in engines, tools, welding, etc.[102]

Most of the boys' lives were immersed in the war, and Susie Monroe's son Norval was killed serving in the U.S. Army under General Patton.

Details on the central blocks are beautifully embroidered. The patriotic theme, most evident in the red, white, and blue, is carried into the shield printed with "God Bless America." The teacher's name, the club name and year, the California poppy, and the names of the boys in the club are all clearly identified. Only the name of the quiltmaker is not listed.

Susie made many quilts and owned family quilts that had been brought from Missouri. This is the only quilt known to have survived.

Sailboats

A group of women in Berkeley formed a sewing club in 1933 for the purpose of catching up on their mending and hemming. After nine years of meetings, one of the members, Elizabeth Rawlings, taught the others how to cut and assemble quilt blocks to make a gift quilt for another member, Margaret Wynkoop Atthowe, who was pregnant. Each contributed a block, including one member's five-year-old daughter, to produce the only quilt made by this group. It was Elizabeth who collected, assembled, and hand-quilted the squares. The group selected a boat pattern to reflect Margaret's husband's family history in navigation.

Margaret's father-in-law, Captain William J. Atthowe, had, as a fourteen-year-old youth, served a four-year apprentice's indenture with a shipping firm in Glasgow, Scotland. The loss of his father at sea in the English Channel in 1891 did not deter William from pursuing a life at sea. By 1895, he and a brother had come to San Francisco, where they worked on the Sacramento delta riverboats of the California Transportation Company, formed by their aunt (an Atthowe) and uncle (Captain Nelson).

The Berkeley Sewing Club that met monthly for forty-nine years: Mary Davis, Ellen Sankey, Edlo Slusser, Margaret Atthowe, Grace Goodfriend, Leah Rehag, and Dottie Williams.

In the mid-1920s, the company ordered two prefabricated steel hulls from Glasgow and built two of the country's finest riverboats, the *Delta King* and the *Delta Queen*. The *Delta Queen* (a historical monument) plies the waters of the Mississippi, and the *Delta King*, moored in Sacramento, is being refurbished as a museum, theater, and hotel. Captain Atthowe commanded the *Delta King*, and his son John was first mate. John left the river in 1939 to marry Margaret Wynkoop, as he did not think the long separations imposed by river work were conducive to a happy marriage.

In 1942, this sailboat quilt, made from the 1936 Kansas City Star pattern, was presented to Margaret. The sewing club met monthly for forty-nine years, from 1933 to 1982.

Sailboats, 1940–1942, made in California. 31 x 48″. Quiltmaker: Sewing Club (coordinated by Elizabeth Rawlings). Collection of Margaret Badgett.

Dresden Plate, Friendship Ring, family name: The Grief Quilt of Nancy Washburn, 1941–1943, made in California. 65″ x 80″. Quiltmaker: Nancy Ellen Susby Washburn (1884–1975). Collection of Elizabeth W. Mayer.

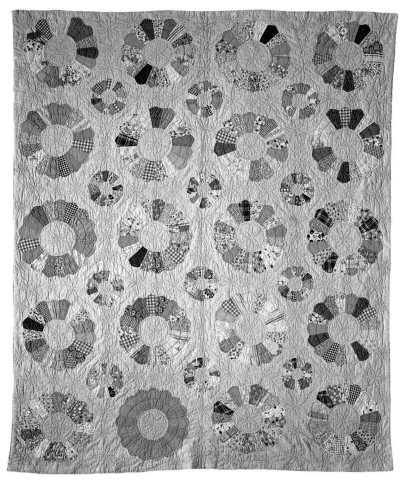

The boats of cotton fabric are hand-quilted in stitches that parallel the pieced lines. The double border is finished with both front and back fabrics turned in and stitched. The quilt is now owned by Margaret's daughter, for whose childhood crib it was intended.

Dresden Plate or Friendship Ring

Nancy Lusby, a motherless child of three or four years, was taken on horseback across Kentucky in 1887 or 1888. According to the family story, Mrs. Barnhill, Nancy's great-aunt, had sent her grown son to see how the children of her deceased niece were being cared for. When they were found alone and without food, he carried the smallest, wrapped in a cover, back to his mother.

Nancy stayed until her tenth or eleventh year, when Mrs. Barnhill died. She then lived with neighbors, the Thompsons, whose own sons were grown and married. As they had never had a daughter, these elderly, loving, and kind people gave her everything she wanted. When she didn't want to go to school, she was hugged and told how glad they were that she wanted to stay with them and watch them quilt.

When Mrs. Thompson died, Nancy, then sixteen, was placed in a church school, where she met Elias Thomas Washburn, both a student and a teacher there. At eighteen, she left school to be married. Ten years her senior, Elias "kept on babying her,"[103] and moved them back to his widowed father's home where the two men grew tobacco. Elias's younger sister, Martha, came to help Nancy, and the two women became devoted friends.

Nancy Ellen Lusby Washburn, maker of the Grief quilt (Dresden Plate Variation), pictured with her husband, Elias Thomas Washburn, on their fiftieth wedding anniversary. 1953.

One day while brushing her hair, Nancy turned to see her father-in-law come into the house holding a black snake in his hands. Nancy ran screaming from the house and refused ever to enter it again. Elias then rented a house in Augusta, Kentucky, gave up farming, and started to sell insurance. Two children were born to them.

In 1909, after twenty-five-year-old Nancy had suffered an illness, they moved to California, a train trip of one week. Her daughter recalls a new wool plaid dress which Nancy made for her. There was a white pinafore apron for each day of the trip.

Nancy's dear friend and sister-in-law, Martha, had died in 1938, leaving five grown children. Three years later, when Martha's youngest son was killed in the attack on Pearl Harbor, Nancy was inconsolable. She declared war on everybody, going window to window in search of enemies, and threatening to take a gun to anybody "who didn't look right."[104] Her grief so overwhelmed her that her husband, desperate to help, recalled that she wanted a quilting frame all their married life, "like they'd had in Kentucky." Her husband would never make one for her. Now he consulted a Mrs. Thompson, who lived next door, asking directions for its construction. Nancy's daughter, Elizabeth, had just taken a job at the local J. C. Penney store. The day the quilt frame was finished, Elizabeth looked up from her station in the yardage department to see her mother walking through the door, perfectly dressed and looking like her old self. Nancy announced that she was going to do a quilt and Elizabeth was to select the fabric, since the quilt was to be for her. Nancy, who had driven herself to the store, was totally recovered!

She placed her quilting frame squarely in the middle of the living room. Mrs. Thompson, the helpful neighbor, informed her that she couldn't use a print on the back of her quilt. In return, Nancy said that her neighbor's stitches were too large. Mrs. Thompson retaliated by telling her they didn't make quilts that way anymore...she recommended that if two sizes of Dresden Plates were to be used, there should be two quilts. Nancy responded: "*This* is the way *this* quilt is going to be made." Elizabeth recalls that they talked this way for the entire week that the quilt was in the frame, and looked forward to it daily.

Elizabeth says, "I understand how my mother was comforted by the pleasure of her childhood while making [the quilt] in a world gone mad....It took her mind to something needing her and back to her loving early home....It saved my mother's reason as well as the reason of the rest of the family. She became normal again after making that quilt."[105]

Elizabeth later heard a talk at the Yuba County Farm Bureau, given by a woman who, with her surgeon-husband, had assisted survivors in Pearl Harbor. She asked the speaker if she had by any chance encountered Sargeant James Derthick, the nephew over whom her mother grieved. The speaker remembered having tended him and offered details of his final days.

Nancy spent years searching for the siblings she had not seen since childhood. Although she was never reunited with her father after her long horseback ride to Mrs. Barnhill's (her great-aunt), he had once brought her a new red lunch pail and left it at the Barnhill house. It was 1951 when her lone brother, the last of the seven children, found her after years of searching, and she was reunited with relatives.

Hand-quilted circles run through the pieced and appliquéd Dresden Plates, and six-petaled flowers (or stars) are repeated throughout this quilt, which now belongs to Nancy's daughter.

Scottie Dog Quilt

Of the five children born to her parents in the town of Ardore, in the territory that would one day become Oklahoma, Louisa was the only survivor. Louisa was a child when her mother died, and she was fourteen or fifteen when her father, a traveling minister, went to preach at a revival in Arkansas, became ill with smallpox, died, and was buried there.

Shortly after, at seventeen, Louisa married William Swader, a farmer and road builder, at the town of Cope in the Indian Territory. She and William traveled often because of his work, building "piked highways" in Oklahoma and Kansas. On one occasion when a road couldn't be finished because of the approaching winter, and it was difficult to take horses back to Oklahoma, they purchased a small hotel, moved into two of the apartments, and rented out the rooms while they awaited spring with their family of two girls and four boys.

When the children were grown, two of them moved to California in search of better jobs during the Depression. Louisa and William followed them, settling near Merced, where they had friends. It was from Merced that Louisa wrote a letter to her daughter Edna Brown. In it, she asked if there was any extra money to help buy fabric for her quilt. Edna sent what she could spare, and the material for the blocks was purchased for thirty-nine cents a yard.

Louisa made many quilts and had always kept her quilting frame hung from the dining room ceiling (where it embarrassed her children).

Louisa Lonesome Barnett Swader, Thousand Oaks, California, in 1941, about a year after completing her Scottie Dogs quilt.

Scottie Dog quilts were inspired during President Franklin D. Roosevelt's administration when he received a Scottie as a gift from a distant relative, his great-aunt's friend Daisy, an eccentric who dyed her hair purple. When Roosevelt mentioned his dog in a speech, its popularity soared. He commented: "Leaders have not been content with attacks on me or my wife or my sons. Now they attack my little dog, Fala." He laughed and the country laughed with him.[106] Scottie dogs appeared everywhere—as toys, or on pillows, decals, pins, and quilts.

Louisa, seeing the Scottie Dog quilt made by a friend, drew her own pattern, matching the original as best she could. Her source for cardboard templates was the back of Big Chief five-cent writing tablets. The pieced Scottie blocks were sewn, embroidered, assembled, and machine-quilted during one cold, rainy winter.

Louisa's sewing was not limited to fabric. Her best shears were pressed into emergency surgery once, on her son's pet chicken, and she was also known to have stitched a dog's ear back together with her needle and thread.

With varying degrees of success, she taught her daughters to quilt, cutting patterns for them from newspapers. Edna made many quilts, but Rene, who managed a small circus and "couldn't make a dress fit to wear,"[107] struggled with

146

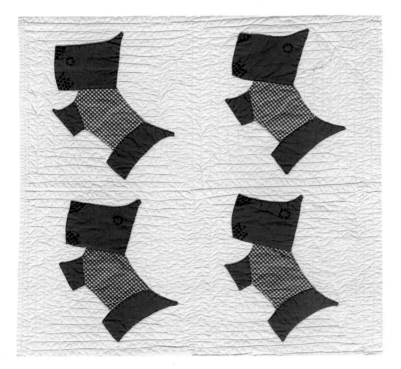

Scottie Dog Quilt, 1940–1945, made in California. 75″ x 83″. Quiltmaker: Louisa Lonesome Barnett Swader (1886–1970). Detail included. Collection of June Huntridge.

a one-patch quilt of machine-pieced pastel fabrics collected from all the women in the family.

Louisa's Scottie Dog quilt is owned by the maker's granddaughter.

Grandmother's Fan

Thousands of "Boomers" joined the land rush into the northern Oklahoma Territory in 1893, where six million acres (purchased from the Cherokees) had been opened for settlement. Among those seeking new lands were Rosalie and her husband, Mr. Rayburn, cotton farmers, whose youngest daughter, Verna, was born the following year, just two months before Rosalie's death.

In 1914, at age twenty, Verna went by herself to California to help her sister with a new baby. She stayed, and in 1917 married Robert R. Young in Upland. They had one son, and after eight years of marriage, Verna was widowed. She then worked as a cotton picker, a fruit packer, and both a domestic and a practical nurse.

It was during World War II, living in Wilmington, California, that she found employment at Douglas Aircraft as a metal-plater, joining about five million other women in the work forces, actively recruited by both government and industry. At that time, she made her Fan quilt. She had started quilting at age six, when she was taught by an older sister and a neighbor. Now, during off hours from her aircraft job, she went back to her quiltmaking, combining old fabrics she had saved with new. She regretted that she was unable to find a different background color—some "prettier, brighter sashings."

Verna died in 1984, having made at least a dozen quilts, including baby quilts. Most were made for her family, but occasionally she was paid for one used as an Eastern Star fund-raiser. This Fan quilt is hand-pieced and hand-quilted in diagonal lines over all the green areas, with outline quilting on the fans.

The present owner, Verna's granddaughter, says the quilt is "a symbol of [her grandmother's] firm belief in the need to use one's time productively, not to be wasteful and to make something practical and lovely with the things one has. It is an illustration of her belief that life is what you make it."

Eyes Aloft Quilt

A pervasive fear that the West Coast was vulnerable to attack by Japanese aircraft predominated in the early years of World War II. Blackouts went into effect and the Aircraft Warning Service was initiated.

The Annette-Choice Valley observation post, near Paso Robles, won special recognition from the National Broadcasting Company in 1942 for its "Eyes Aloft" program. A gold trophy was presented by Captain Droege (standing in for General W. E. Kepner) for the post's one hundred percent record, maintaining a spotter on duty at all times. Because the community was small, each volunteer had a minimum of one six-hour turn each week. They watched for planes, day and night, and when one was spotted, a call was made to the Fourth Fighter Command (one long ring and three short) to report its direction and identification. The spotters were equally busy with scrap metal; they collected sixty-two tons, for which they were also commended. The formal presentation was followed by a chicken dinner that was cooked by the women in the community.

Mary Grant recognized the patriotic devotion of the spotters with a commemorative quilt that she made for Theadore Twisselman, who was in charge of the local Aircraft Warning Service. Born Mary Smith in 1898 in Broomfield, Colorado, she lived in California at the time of her second marriage to Fred Grant, a rancher. Their home was in the country in Bitter Water Valley, near Chalome, when she undertook this forty-star quilt. Mother of three sons, she wrote and

Certificate awarded to Eleanora Twisselman by the Air Force for her 773 hours "on the alert." She was the mother of the chief observer for the Eyes Aloft airplane spotter's program. 1942.

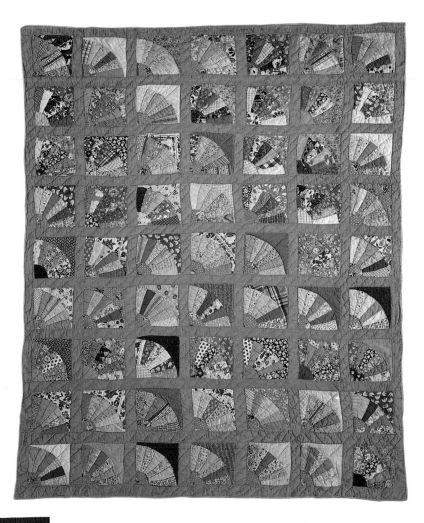

Grandmother's Fan, family name:
Fantan, 1940–1945, made in California. 73″ x 92″. Quiltmaker:
Verna Alice Rayburn Young (1894–
1984). Collection of Nancy Smith.

Eyes Aloft Quilt, 1942–1944, made
in California. 65″ x 98″. Quiltmaker: Mary Smith Landry Grant
(1898–1976). Collection of Frank
and Pat Twisselman.

embroidered all the names of the "Eyes Aloft" spotters in white on the blue stars. At the center of the quilt, embroidered in red, are the names of the men from that community who were in military service.

Mary's son recalls that an old quilting frame was renovated for this project and set up in the living room, where his mother quilted with friends and neighbors in the afternoons, while the light was good. She was a "lovely, public-spirited woman," stated a friend. "Always baking cakes for community doings and functions."

The stars are blind-stitch appliquéd to the white squares, which are machine-pieced. Outline quilting follows the blocks and stars, all bordered in patriotic stripes. The present owner of the quilt is a son of Theadore Twisselman, for whom the quilt was made.

Mary Smith Landry Grant, who made the Eyes Aloft quilt, pictured with her son, Al Landry, his wife, Eunice, and their daughter, Bobbie Jo.

Notes

1. *Antiques* magazine, November 1931.
2. Florence H. Pettit, *America's Indigo Blues* (New York: Hastings House, 1974), 195.
3. Florence H. Pettit, *America's Printed and Painted Fabrics, 1600–1900* (New York: Hastings House, 1970), 102–105.
4. Florence M. Montgomery, *Printed Textiles* (New York: Viking, 1970), 209.
5. Pettit, *America's Indigo Blues*, 133.
6. Francis Deirne, *The Amiable Baltimoreans* (New York: E. P. Dutton, 1951), 82.
7. Henry Fletcher Powell, comp., *The Tercentenary History of Maryland*, vol. 4 (Chicago: Clarke Publishing, 1925), 888.
8. Written interview with owner, 1986.
9. Harvey G. Schlichter, *Two Centuries of Grace and Growth in Manchester* (Westminster, Md.: Opera House Printing, 1960), 33.
10. Ibid., 36.
11. Thomas C. Savage, "Times Gone By in Alta, California," 1878, p. 2, Manuscript in the Bancroft Library, University of California, Berkeley.
12. Ibid., p. 7.
13. Ibid., p. 8.
14. Ibid., p. 2.
15. Joan M. Jensen and Gloria Ricci Lothrop, *California Women: A History* (San Francisco: Boyd and Fraser, 1987), 16.
16. Letter from Anna Zerissa Morse Thurston to her mother, Emily Hammond Morse, April 30, 1862.
17. Ibid., September 19, 1869.
18. Ibid., August 21, 1871.
19. Ibid., October 23, 1871.
20. Ibid., (exact date unknown).
21. Ibid., November 16, 1872.
22. Ibid., January 11, 1874.
23. Ibid., April 14, 1874.
24. Ibid., January 8, 1883.
25. Letter from Sallie E. Wade to Eugene Thurston, 1886 (exact date unknown).
26. Mary Twist, *Just an Ordinary Family* (Minneapolis: Osterhus, n.d.), 8.
27. Ibid.
28. Ibid., 22.
29. Carolyn Cotter Klemeyer, written interview, 1987.
30. Ibid.
31. Letter from Jeanette E. Cameron Ayres to Georgie Stanley Ayres Smith and family, 1902.
32. Allen M. Trout, "Greetings: Allen M. Trout," *Louisville (Kentucky) Courier-Journal*, August 20, 1955, n.p.
33. Ibid.
34. Mrs. Edwina Allen Atterbury, written interview, May 1986.
35. Ibid.
36. Bettina Havig, *Missouri Heritage Quilts* (Paducah, Ky.: American Quilters Society, 1986), 12.
37. Henrietta Reynolds, *Pioneers of Sand-Plains in San Joaquin County, California* (San Francisco (?): Author, 1953), 16.
38. Ibid.
39. Ibid., 34.
40. Ibid., 13.
41. The spoons are displayed in a memorial case at the Pioneer Museum in Stockton, California.
42. *Christie's* 10 (December 1988), n.p.
43. Written recollection (date unknown) by Wesley Davis of his wife, Mary Lutisha (Rice) Davis, the granddaughter of Mary Beck.
44. The Book Club of California, *The Panama Canal: The Evolution of the Isthmian Crossing*, Keepsake Series (San Francisco: The Book Club of California, 1965).
45. Mildred Breitbarth, written interview, 1985.
46. Granger Family Booklet, 1931 (?).
47. Letter from Elizabeth Peterman to her daughter, Catherine Peterman Thomas Plymire, dated September 20. (No year is given; estimated in the early 1860s.)
48. Letter from Mary Jane Thomas to her daughter Katherine Amanda Thomas (later Simpson), dated January 21. (No year is given; estimated in the early 1870s.)
49. Ed Mannion, "Rear-View Mirror," newspaper article (no further identification available), 1963.
50. The Book Club of California, *The Panama Canal: The Evolution of the Isthmian Crossing*, Keepsake Series, (San Francisco: The Book Club of California, 1965).
51. Ibid.

52. *San Francisco Chronicle*, May 1988, n.p.
53. John Duffy, "Military Medicine: The Civil War," in *The Healers: The Rise of the Medical Establishment* (New York: McGraw-Hill, 1976), 270.
54. Ibid., 223.
55. Ibid.
56. George Washington's stepchildren, one of whom was Robert E. Lee's bride, were Custises.
57. Evelyn Pearl (McIntyre) Joslyn, *One Woman's California* (Oroville, Calif.: Hironimus Press, 1984), 26.
58. Ruth Plumstead, written interview, 1986 or 1987.
59. D. G. Hall, "The Memoirs of D. G. Hall," typewritten manuscript, 1937, p. 7.
60. Ibid.
61. Ibid.
62. Letter from Bertha Eldora Osborn to Harriet Houston's mother, September 26, 1936.
63. Leona Galley, written interview, 1988.
64. Rofena Polk, written interview, September 1986.
65. Dorothy Cozart, "When the Smoke Clears," *Quilt Digest* 5 (1987):51.
66. "Action Answers," *The Fresno Bee*, June 21, 1979.
67. Elisabeth E. Basore, written interview, January 1987.
68. Myrna Raglin, written interview, 1988.
69. Cuesta Benberry, "The 20th Century's First Quilt Revival," *Quilters' Newsletter*, October 1979, n.p.
70. "One Thousand Dollars for the Red Cross Can Be Raised on a Memorial Quilt," *The Modern Priscilla*, December 1917, 2.
71. John E. Baur, *Health Seekers of Southern California* (San Marino, Calif.: Huntington Library, 1959), 14.
72. Hazel Sawyer, telephone interview, September 1988.
73. Sadie Bartal, telephone interview, October 1988.
74. Ibid.
75. John W. Robinson, *The Mount Wilson Story* (Glendale, Calif.: LaSiesta Press, 1973), 10.
76. Ibid.
77. Joyce Beaty, written interview, 1988.
78. Ibid.
79. Vera Camp Glendenning, written interview, 1986.
80. Linda Gilfillan McAlexander, written interview, 1986.
81. Ibid.
82. M. J. Van Natta, written interview, 1988.
83. Gladys Killion, written interview, 1986.
84. Gladys Killion, telephone interview, October 1988.
85. Robin Guzman, written interview, 1988.
86. Ibid.
87. Wendy Eads, written interview, 1986.
88. Ibid.
89. Ibid.
90. Martha Fields, written interview, 1987.
91. James Collord, telephone interview, November 1988.
92. John Bidwell, *A Journey to California* (San Francisco: n.p., 1937), 44.
93. Emma S. Tyrell, "The Lone Eagle Quilt," *Successful Farming*, January 1929, 48.
94. Pat Nickols, telephone interview. Nickols has researched the use of bags in quilts.
95. Ruby Vise, telephone interview, October 1988.
96. Vincent Bezdecheck, written interview, 1988.
97. Vincent Bezdecheck, telephone interview, November 1988.
98. Vincent Bezdecheck, written interview, 1988.
99. *Stephens College Alumnae News Bulletin*, February 1937, 1.
100. Helen G. MacIntosh, written interview, March 7, 1988.
101. Letter from Helen G. MacIntosh to Virginia McElroy, March 7, 1988.
102. Roberta Suiter Chapin, written interview, 1985.
103. Elizabeth Mayer, taped interview, 1988.
104. Ibid.
105. Ibid.
106. James Roosevelt (with Bill Libby), *My Parents: A Differing View* (Chicago: Playboy Press, 1976), 168.
107. Edna Brown, telephone interview, October 1988.